KU-739-449

THE SOUL OF THE
WHITE ANT

BOOKS BY
Eugène N. Marais

Versamelde Werke 1
Versamelde Werke 2
The Soul of the Ape
Dwaalstories

THE SOUL OF THE WHITE ANT

EUGÈNE N. MARAIS

With a biographical note by his son

Translated by
Winifred de Kok

HUMAN & ROUSSEAU
Cape Town Pretoria

The publishers are gratefully indebted to W.V. Harris for his help
and for supplying photographs and to
Rentokil Laboratories for their assistance.

First published in Afrikaans under the title *Die Siel van die Mier*, 1937
First edition in English 1970 by Human & Rousseau

All rights reserved
This edition published in 2006 by Human & Rousseau,
a division of NB Publishers (Pty) Limited,
40 Heerengracht, Cape Town, 8001 (Head office)
1064 Arcadia Street, Pretoria, 0083
Cover design by Flame Design
Typography by Etienne van Duyker
Set in 11.5 on 15.5 pt Berkeley Book by Alinea Studio, Cape Town
Printed and bound by Paarl Print, Oosterland Street, Paarl, South Africa

ISBN-10: 0-7981-4593-5
ISBN-13: 978-0-7981-4593-0

No part of this book may be reproduced or transmitted in any form
or by any electronic or mechanical means, including photcopying and
recording, or by any other information storage or retrieval system,
without written permission from the publisher

Contents

Translator's Preface

The name of Eugène N. Marais is known to all Afrikaans-speaking South Africans as a writer of short stories and verse. He himself, however, would wish to be remembered for his lifelong study of termites and apes. He began life after leaving college as a journalist, then studied medicine for four years, but eventually took up law and was called to the Bar by the Inner Temple. A scholar and a man of culture, he chose nevertheless to live for a period extending over many years in a "rondhavel" or hut in the lonely Waterberg mountains, learning to know and make friends with a troop of wild baboons, whose behaviour he wished to study. He tamed them to such a degree that he could move among them and handle them with impunity. At the same time he busied himself with the other end of the chain and studied termite life, a study which often meant tremendous drudgery and needed endless patience.

During those years Eugène Marais was not concerned with publicity in any form, but a friend induced him to write an article for an Afrikaans periodical called *Die Huisgenoot*. This proved so popular that the author was besieged for more, and the articles continued for almost two years.

His years of unceasing work on the veld led Eugène Marais to formulate his theory that the individual nest of the termites is similar in every respect to the organism of an animal, workers and soldiers resembling red and white blood corpuscles, the fungus gardens the digestive organs, the queen functioning as the brain, and the sexual flight being in every respect analogous to the escape of spermatozoa and ova.

About six years after these articles appeared, Maurice Maeterlinck published his book, *The Life of the White Ant,* in which he describes this organic unity of the termitary and compares it with the human body. This theory aroused great interest at the time and was generally accepted as an original one formulated by Maeterlinck. The fact that an unknown South African observer had developed the theory after many years of indefatigable labour was not generally known in Europe. Excerpts from Marais' articles had, however, appeared in both the Belgian and the French press at the time of their publication in South Africa. Indeed, the original Afrikaans articles would have been intelligible to any Fleming, for Afrikaans and Flemish are very similar.

No one who reads this book, based on the articles published so many years earlier than Maeterlinck's book, will hesitate to give its author the honour due to him.

Eugène Marais intended writing a fuller and more scientific volume, but this intention was frustrated by his untimely death.

WINIFRED DE KOK

EUGÈNE N. MARAIS
A biographical note by his son

Eugène Nielen Marais was born on January 9, 1872 in Pretoria. He was the son of Jan Christian Nielen Marais of Stellenbosch, who traced his descent through a few generations to a Charles Marais, a French Huguenot. Into this family had married Baron van Rheede van Oudtshoorn, who had been sent out to be Governor of the Cape and who had died on board ship in Table Bay, and Dr. Nielen, an American doctor who had come out to South Africa.

Eugène Marais received his first definite schooling in English from an Archdeacon Roberts in Pretoria in which school he won a "prize for divinity" because he could recite the whole of the Catechism of the Church of England. After a journey by ox-wagon through the bushveld he was taken to Boshof in the Orange Free State, where he again went to an English school and later to the Paarl.

At the end of the 1880s he was back in Pretoria and in a few years seemed definitely to have adopted journalism as his profession. At first he was a parliamentary reporter of the Volksraad and because of his caustic comments on the proceedings he had the distinction of being expressly excluded from the press gallery by a resolution of the Volksraad. He became Editor of various papers, both English and Dutch, and his whole-hearted support of General Joubert against Kruger resulted in his being tried for high treason, on which charge he was acquitted by the Supreme Court in Pretoria. During this period of his residence in Pretoria he showed great interest in animals and insects and was never without tame apes, snakes, scorpions, and the like. In 1894 he married Miss L. Beyers in Natal, but lost his wife the following year. The loss of his wife had a profound effect on him and accentuated the sombre side of his nature which had already occasionally clouded an otherwise bright-spirited temperament.

In 1895 he left for Europe with the intention of studying medicine, but he was persuaded by friends in the Transvaal to take up law. He made the change, much to his subsequent regret, and at the Inner Temple in London qualified as an advocate. He studied medicine at the same time, however, and only the Boer War prevented him from qualifying. He was on parole in England during the Boer War until an opportunity offered itself of going on an expedition to Central Africa, from where he intended to take medical supplies and explosives which he had collected to the Boer Forces across the Limpopo. While still in Central Africa, where he contracted a severe attack of malaria fever, he heard of the conclusion of peace 1902 – the stores and supplies were buried and he returned to Pretoria via Delagoa Bay. During his travels he had added greatly to his store of knowledge about the habits of insects and animals.

In Pretoria he began to practise as an advocate and produced a book on Deeds Office Practice. He was still interested in his newspaper *Land and Volk,* for which he wrote in what was considered "Afrikaans". His poem "Winternag" heralded the new Afrikaans movement.

In 1910 Marais went to Johannesburg, where he again practised as an advocate, but his distaste for the work, coupled with increasing depression of spirits, made him give up his practice and move to the Waterberg district. There he made an intensive study of birds and beasts. There was no natural phenomenon which came amiss to his eager mind and he wrote an article for the Government Agricultural Journal on the drying up of Waterberg which was reproduced by the Smithsonian Institute in their annual report. At the same time he was contributing articles on snake poison and stories to the Afrikaans press.

In the district he freely gave of his medical knowledge to help the poverty-stricken population and acted for years as Justice of the Peace.

But by the end of 1915 his health was so bad that he had to have careful attention, and he was taken to Pretoria, with the happy result that after some months he was able to resume his practice as an advocate. He had chambers near and was a close friend of the late Mr. Tielman Roos. There was again a period of literary activity, but constantly failing health made him give up his practice and then followed a period of practice as an attorney at Bronkhorstspruit and Heidelberg in the Transvaal. By this time he had completed the draft of what he hoped would be his chief work – *The Soul of the Ape* – a study of the behaviour of apes and baboons and the comparison of their mental processes, as far as these could be gauged, with those of man.

His delight now was to use the new-fledged Afrikaans as a medium of expression, and the opening it offered for the coming of new words and modes of expression was eagerly seized by him. And while poems, stories and articles flowed from his pen for newspaper and magazine in Afrikaans, he contributed to English scientific journals in English.

Again in 1928 a breakdown in health brought him to Pretoria, where he kept up his journalistic work and endeavoured to give form to his work on the termites and ants. There is much that he would have added and possibly much that he would have corrected in the present work had his health permitted him to give undivided attention to the work. But it was not to be, and on March 29, 1936 he died on a farm near Pretoria.

Of a singularly attractive nature he was adored by and adored children and especially in his later years could almost always be found in their company. He has a clear and assured niche among the most-noted writers in Afrikaans, and his scientific work and theories written in English have received special notice in America and Europe.

LIST OF ILLUSTRATIONS

1

THE BEGINNING OF A TERMITARY

Some years ago an article about "white ants", as termites are commonly but incorrectly called, appeared in a South African journal. Almost everything that naturalists tell us about these insects is important and interesting, and Dr. Hesse's article was exceptionally so. But the article also made another fact clear; how very little is done in our land to study the behaviour of animals, and how much has been done and is being done in other countries. Everything that Dr. Hesse told us was the result of long and patient observation in America and Europe. None of his facts was exactly relevant to our South African termites.

The life-history of most of our South African ants and termites is in every respect just as wonderful and interesting as anything that has been discovered in South America. Over a period of ten years I studied the habits of termites in an investigation into animal psychology. I then realized that such observation reveals new wonders every day. To mention one instance, the functioning of the community or group-psyche of the termitary is just as wonderful and mysterious to a human being, with a very different kind of psyche, as telepathy or other functions of the human mind which border on the supernatural.

When one wishes to write of all these wonders, one is bewildered by the *embarras de richesses*. It is hard to know where to begin.

I want to tell you about the commonest of our termites or "white ants", and what I am going to relate may be observed by anyone who wishes; he may even discover new wonders. Most of these facts have not been published before; indeed, I do not think they have been discovered by scientists.

The common termite which is so destructive to wood of all kinds, and builds "ant-hills" or termitaries on the open veld, is known throughout South Africa. I will tell you a little about the beginning of its community life.

The beginning of a termitary dates from the moment when the termites fly, after rain and usually at dusk, in order to escape their innumerable enemies. Even here we see a remarkable instance of the wonder of instinct. The termites beginning their thrilling flight know nothing about enemies. They have never been outside the nest before. The peril of existence is to them a closed book, and yet nine times out of ten they do not fly until the birds are safely in their nests.

These flying termites are at least twenty times as big as the others of the nest, and quite different in colour and form. You must consider a termitary as a single animal, whose organs have not yet been fused together as in a human being. Some of the termites form the mouth and digestive system; others take the place of weapons of defence like claws or horns; others form the generative organs. These flying termites are the generative organs of the colony. Every one of these winged insects is a potential king or queen. The four beautiful wings have taken months to develop and grow to perfection; months elapse – or even years in very dry districts – before an opportunity for flight occurs. They will never fly until there has been rain, and the reason is obvious. After the flight they must seek immediate shelter in the ground, and when the ground is hard and dry this is impossible.

Follow the flight of the termites carefully from the moment they emerge from the nest. They crawl out of a little opening, thousand upon thousand. There is obviously much excitement in the termitary. Sometimes the flyers are escorted to the opening by workers and soldiers. The first impulse of the flying insect as it emerges is to try its wings. It flutters and essays to lift itself into the air. If it fails, it climbs a grass stalk and takes off from this height. But fly it must, even if it is only for a few inches. You will understand presently why this is so essential, just as necessary as the preservation of its life, and therefore it takes just as much trouble to fly – even more perhaps, for the urge is greater – as to protect itself from enemies.

The watcher will soon become aware that the object of the flight seems to be to spread the insects over as large an area as possible, as some plants disseminate their seed. Some of the termites rise high into the air and travel for miles before they settle; others sink to the ground only a stride or two from the old nest. But far or near, fly they must, or the sole object of their existence is frustrated.

Let us watch one of the ants which has flown and settled in the grass near at hand. We will suppose it is female – the two sexes cannot be distinguished with the naked eye. The first thing she does is to discard her wings. This she succeeds in doing by a lightening-like movement – so fast that we cannot follow it with the eye. One moment we see her with her wings intact, the next moment she steps away, and her four wings are

Soldier and worker termites.

lying on the grass – she is much, much quicker than a woman who discards her evening gown and hangs it over a chair. It took months for her wings to grow. For years perhaps she has lived in subterranean darkness, in preparation for this one moment. For a period of three seconds, for a distance of per-

18

Winged adult termites.

haps three yards, she enjoyed the exquisite thrill of flight and with that the object of a great preparation has been fulfilled and the fairy-like wings are flung aside like a worn-out garment.

Immediately the wings are discarded she walks about rapidly for a few seconds. You become aware that she is seeking a suitable place for some further purpose – but you do not know what the purpose can be, and her immediate behaviour does not clear things up for you. You must watch patiently if you wish to discover what she intends doing. When she has found a suitable spot, she does a very peculiar thing. She comes to rest on her fore-feet and lifts three-quarters of the hinder part of her body into the air, and she remains stationary in this position, as still as if she were merely the statue of a termite. If you become impatient and walk away the secret

19

Female termites after shedding their wings.

of the flying termite will remain a secret to you for ever. What is she doing? She is busy sending a wireless S.O.S. into the air. Be patient a little longer – there are only very few people who have witnessed this miracle. What does the signal consist of?

I *think* I know, but I doubt if you will guess what it is. Only if you have made a study of the signals of insects will you find the clue. You think, of course, of some sound which cannot be heard by the human ear. You may know how our little South African *toktokkie** beetle knocks in similar circumstances. No, the termite's signal is not a sound. One can prove that by experiment. We will content ourselves for the moment with the fact that the signal consists of something far and away beyond our

* A beetle of the genus *Psammodes*.

20

own senses, and yet the male becomes aware of it over incredible distances! How does this happen? Well, it *does* happen, and our female is a very modern young woman, not too shy to make the first move in love-making. If you wait long enough you will presently see another termite come flying through the air, and you will notice that although his flight appears awkward and almost involuntary, yet he can steer a course and choose a direction even against the wind. The male sinks to the ground sometimes a yard or two from the place where the female is standing motionless in her curious posture. As soon as he lands he makes the same lightening-like movement which we have already seen in the female, and there on the ground lie his wings, too. His haste is terrible and irresistible. Over and through the grass he crawls, so fast that we can barely follow him with our eyes. He is looking for the originator of the signal which he received high up in the air. Within a few minutes he has found her. She has been motionless all the while, with her body hoisted aloft, but the instant the male touches her with his antennae, he infects her with his own excitement. She begins to run away as fast as her legs will carry her, and immediately behind her comes the male. They are now beginning the final search – they are house-hunting, and this the male leaves to his wife. It must be a good house, for they will live in if for a long time. And with the finding of their home and the digging of the front door we will leave the happy pair for a while.

There are even stranger things connected with this little drama, of which the inexperienced observer will not become aware. I spoke of the urge to flight. Listen carefully. If those two termites had not flown, none of the events we have watched would have occurred. Instinct is something which only works step by step. If you destroy one step or omit it, then the whole thing collapses. Nature wishes the "white ant" to spread. If the nests are too close together it would be bad for the communities; therefore they receive wings and must fly. But flight is only one step in their sexual life; if this step is omitted, their sexual life and their very existence ends there and then.

For as long as two years the two sexes may live in the same nest after they have grown wings. They are in constant touch with each other but there is not the least evidence of any sexual life. They *must* crawl out of the nest, they must fly, must settle and lose their wings, then and then only, and then immediately, sexual life begins. If you prevent them flying and break off the wings, both male and female die without any further attempt to become progenitors of the race. The length and distance of the flight is of no importance; it may last hours or only a second; it may cover miles or only an inch. But the force which we call instinct commands – you *must* pass through every stage, you must take every step, or you are doomed. If you take a male and female just as they are emerging from the nest and place them beside each other, even in the closest contact, you notice that they take not the least interest in each other. They struggle to get away from each other. Let the female fly a few inches and the whole process which we described is carried out to a finish. Let the male circle round even once, then force him to land near the female, then and then alone, will events take their normal course. A second in time, three inches in space, one flutter of wings, are to the termite a gulf as wide as infinity dividing two kinds of existence. To us it may appear only a small dividing line, but the insect *may* not overstep it, not even with human assistance.

22

2

UNSOLVED SECRETS

There is much to be told about the building of the termitary, but I will confine myself to behaviour which is important for purposes of comparison. All behaviour is of importance to the psychologist. Behaviour *is* psychology – at least it is all of the psyche we know or can study. For purposes of comparison, for comparative psychology – especially if you begin at the top of the ladder with the apes – the field at our disposal is not very large.

Upon the king and queen themselves falls the task of feeding and attending to the first children. After the latter are full-grown they take upon themselves all the work of the community. In the meantime the queen grows larger and fatter by the hour. Her small neat body vanishes in increasing layers of fat until at last it becomes an unsightly wormlike bag of adiposity. And to heighten the tragedy, her mate, in addition to having the blessing of almost the only *dolce far niente* existence known to nature, appears to have discovered the secret of eternal youth. He remains as beautiful and active and young as he was on his wedding flight. But if you look at her, an immovable disgusting worm, it seems impossible to believe that she ever fluttered in the air on fairy wings. We could hardly blame his majesty if he began casting an eye at some other female a little less repellent. If you fear this, however, you will be pleasantly surprised. His attachment to his queen seems to keep pace with her own growth. If you lay open the palace cavity, he rushes round in consternation, but always returns to her side. There is no question of saving his own life in flight. He clings to her gigantic body and tries to defend it, and if the ruthless attacker so wills, he dies at her side. What a wonderful example of married love and fidelity, which can survive this terrible change of his beloved to a loathsome mass of fat!

We often speak metaphorically of a queen as the mother of her people. This the termite queen is literally. She is the only mother of the millions which form the community; every individual is born out of her. Naturally she is absolved from all duty in the nursery. All she is expected to do is to keep on laying an endless stream of eggs, because the daily loss of workers and soldiers is enormous, notwithstanding their excellent methods of defence. Mother Nature is not perturbed about the death of a thousand individuals, when she has had the foresight to make certain of an unending supply.

I am now coming to a stage when in actuality every termitary differs in its growth, but for our purpose we will suppose that the environment of our nest has been such that development is entirely normal and not subjected to any disturbing outside influences. The first workers begin to build a palace for the queen. Deep below the surface of the earth, from three to six feet, they prepare a hollow chamber. As years go by this is gradually increased in size, and the earth which is excavated is taken to the surface and used to form the thick defensive crust. In this hollow chamber the queen is placed. It fits her so well that one is inclined to think that it has been built around her. I do not think this actually happens, but now I come to a stage when almost every conclusion is bound to be mere guess-work. No human eye has ever seen what actually takes place. No one has ever discovered a way in which to watch the termites at work in the queen's chamber, for they work in pitch darkness and to let light into the chamber is as great a handicap to the termites as the sudden destruction of the sun would be to us. *We* cannot see in complete darkness.

The queen continues growing until, compared with the ordinary termite, she reaches a gigantic size, and becomes an immobile mass, still as a log. The only part of her which gives any sign of life is the little head, which remains unchanged. If you dissect the skin and body carefully and examine it under a microscope, you will be convinced that during her later stages of growth the queen is unable to make any voluntary movement, except of course of the head.

You may think she could move like some worms do, by contraction and expansion. But you will find that no part of the body behind the head can be controlled by what was once an intricate central nervous system. Nor do I think that there can be any question of her regaining the power of movement temporarily, as for instance by emptying the sac for a while. I certainly have seen no indication of this. Besides, the very nerves in the body have changed into fluid. Both these theories, therefore, that the queen is able to move by contraction and expansion, or that she gains a temporary power of movement, must be discarded.

To continue with the queen's life-history, her first palace is a cell made of termite earth which rapidly becomes as hard as

25

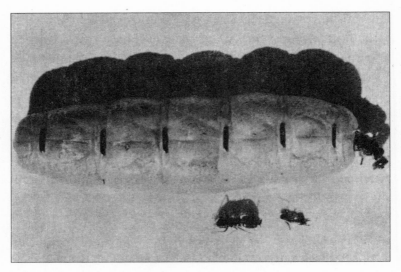

A queen termite full of eggs with two soldier termites.

cement. Usually she just neatly fits into it. She is always much too huge to use the door of the cell as entrance or exit. If you wish to remove her you must break down the cell. The king and the workers, however, can come and go quite easily. She is fed and the eggs which she never ceases laying are removed to the breeding grounds by workers appointed to this task. The king apparently does nothing. He appears to be a mere hanger-on in the palace. Still the queen goes on growing. Here in her first palace she has not attained one-third of her eventual size. At last she very nearly fills all the available space in the cell. There is barely room for the tiny workers to carry the eggs away across the insensate bulk. A terrible tragedy appears to be imminent – it reminds us of the question: what will happen if an irresistible force meets an immovable mass? The human observer is helpless at the threat of this terrible

26

fate. In spite of all his knowledge and intelligence he is unable to help in any way. But actually termites have never worried about it at all. They had a solution ready – a very simple one. Just before her majesty finally outgrows her cell they build a second one, one and a half times as big as the first. It is parallel and adjacent to the first, just as hard and with just such a narrow door. The queen is then removed and placed in the second cell where there is space for her to grow for perhaps another year. So she gets transposed from cell to cell until there have been about six changes with the queen in the last and biggest. The chamber doors are always equally small – much too small for the queen to come or go by.

We must clearly establish another fact which makes the whole matter even more complicated. One could easily prove by measurement that the queen's subjects could not possibly move her. The lifting power of one termite can be estimated fairly closely, and the area of the queen's body available for workers to grasp during lifting can be measured. During the later stages it would need thousands more termites to lift her than there is available grasping space for on the body.

We present to you the following facts:
1. The queen is incapable of movement.
2. The doors of the cell are too small for her to come or go by.
3. The insects cannot lift her.
4. Yet she vanishes from one cell to appear in another.

The only explanation that seems feasible is that there are several queens and that it is not the same one each time. If the first gets too big for her cell, she is killed and eaten and then the workers carry a potential queen into the second cell where she develops into a queen. The only intelligent explanation, perhaps, and very simple, now we have thought of it. The only pity is that it is not true. We have been deceived by the analogy of the bees, which make queens, kill, and move them. It is quite an easy matter to mark the termite queen and so prove that it is the same queen which gets moved. I have tested many theories brought forward by friends who have studied entomology, but have never found one which coincided with all the facts. Perhaps one day a future Fabre will discover the truth.

3

LANGUAGE IN THE INSECT WORLD

I have told you how, shortly after she discards her wings, the flying queen sends a signal into the air, which is always answered by the appearance of a male flying through the air. What exactly the signal was I did not make clear, but left it for some later opportunity. I want to talk about it now. But I am afraid there will be a long preface before I begin — perhaps the preface may take even this whole chapter. The inquisitive reader need not be disappointed, however, for I am sure this preface will prove interesting, too. In order to understand the language of animals, one must first of all learn it's A B C, but of far more importance are the things you must unlearn. We will therefore begin at the very beginning.

An individual member of any animal race which wishes to communicate with another at a distance can use one of three things; colour, scent or sound. And at this point you must begin unlearning. If you think of colour and scent and sound in terms of the impression which these make on a human being, then you will be lost before you begin your journey. Listen. There is one kind of termite which constantly signals by means of sounds. If ever you have slept in a house in which

29

those termites are at work you will know the sound well. It is a quick tik-tik-tik. You can also hear this if you let down a microphone through a hole made into an termitary. You will easily observe that not only do the termites make this noise, but that other termites at a distance hear it and immediately react to it by their behaviour.

Now catch one or more of the signallers and examine their anatomy under the microscope. What do you find? Not the least sign or suggestion of any kind of auditory organ; not even the most primitive kind of ear; not a single nerve that could possibly be sensitive to what we call sound. We find the same as regards colour and scent. The termites undoubtedly use both colour and scent as a means of signalling – as you will see later. But again you seek in vain for any organ resembling an eye. There is not even the faintest spot of pigment which might serve as a primitive eye. The termites are quite blind, yet sensitive to an indirect ray of light far below the threshold of perception of the human eye. By this I mean they can become aware of a very diffuse light not shining directly on them, which a human eye could not perceive. This can be proved by experiment. As to any organ of smell, that, too, seems to be completely absent.

Let us now observe another insect, our dear little *toktokkie* beetle, which will take us a good way along the path we must travel, and will greatly help to explain the secret to us. If you wish to learn to know the *toktokkie* really well and to learn to talk his language, you *must* tame him. He must become so used to your presence that he never alters his behaviour by suddenly becoming aware of being observed. He is very easy to tame, at least the grey-bellied one is, and learns to know his master and love him – you know the one I mean, the smooth little fellow with pale legs, not the rough-backed one. What South African child has never seen the *toktokkie* and heard him make his knock? Your eye suddenly falls on him in the road or beside it. If he does not get a fright and fall down dead with stiff legs – as dead as the deadest *toktokkie* which ever lived – then you see him knock, and of course hear him, too. He looks round for some hard object, a piece of earth or a stone, and knocks against it with the last segment of his body – three, four, four, three! This is his Morse Code. He then listens for a moment or two, turning rapidly in many directions. His behaviour is ridiculously human. His whole body becomes an animated question mark. You can almost hear him saying:

"I'm positive I heard her knock! Where can she be? There, I hear it again!"

He answers with three hard knocks, and then he betakes himself off in great haste and runs a yard or two. He then repeats the signal in order to get a further true direction, and so he continues until at last he arrives at his loved one's side.

If you study the behaviour of many *toktokkies* during the mating season, you will occasionally have to follow one for an incredible distance in the direction of the answering signal. He can hear the signal over a distance which makes the sound absolutely imperceptible to the human ear. It is at this stage that he begins to rouse the interest of the psychologist. We study him at closer quarters. Again we find under the microscope no sign of an ear, nor complex or nerve which takes the place of an organ of hearing. But in spite of this we still think of the behaviour of the *toktokkie* in terms of sound and hearing!

Now we will go into our laboratory with our tame *toktokkies*. The laboratory is a stretch of natural veld or a fairly large garden. The observer will soon discover that the *toktokkie* is one of the most credulous of insects. When he is dominated by sexual desire, he will believe everything you happen to tell him. Knock on a stone with your fingernail – in his own Morse Code – and at once he answers. You can teach him quite easily never to knock except in answer to your signal. This you succeed in doing by not knocking for several days unless he has become perfectly quiet. After a day or two he will have learnt to knock only in answer to your signal – and will answer immediately. Now get a small microphone with headpiece and three feet of wire (you will find this indispensable in your association with the insect world). The microphone must be so powerful that you are able to hear the footfall of a fly quite easily. When your *toktokkie* is tame and well trained you proceed to test the acuteness of his perceptions. To your amazement you find that they are unbelievably, supernaturally fine. Knock on the stone again with your finger-nail and gradually make the sound softer until it is quite beyond your own hearing. Still the *toktokkie* answers the signal at once without the least sign of doubt. Then begin knocking not with the nail but with the soft pulp of the finger. There seems to be no sound at all, but still the *toktokkie* answers! Now take the microphone and place it on the ground with the earphones over your ears. Knock on the receiver with the pulp of your finger – a real knock, not merely a pressure. With a little practice you can reduce the sound until at last it is inaudible even through the micro-phone, but still the *toktokkie* hears it!

The solution to this problem is: It is not sound as such which the *toktokkie* becomes aware of, and there can be no question of *hearing* it. Any book of physiology will make it clear to you that sound is only our interpretation of certain vibrations in the atmosphere. (Sound cannot travel through a vacuum – you can prove this by sending a sound through a wire inserted in the cork of a thermos flask. It will be imperceptible, except for a faint noise which escapes through the cork.) It is our ear which interprets the vibrations as sound. Beyond the ear the universe is soundless. Without an ear – or organ of hearing – there can be no sound. But the vibrations which we call sound have a physical function. It is by the exercise of physical force that the drum of the ear and the hammer and anvil bones of the inner ear are set into vibration. In the same way you can let grains of sand or a thin gas-flame vibrate to a musical note. But there is another difficulty. The sudden meeting of the surfaces of two physical bodies can result in vibrations of the mysterious ether, which are not by any means sound-waves and therefore have no effect at all on our ears. We are getting into somewhat deep water now. I believe it is vibrations of this kind, waves in the ether, of which the ants and the *toktokkie* make use. It may sound far-fetched, but you will have to accept some such expla-nation if you wish to learn the language of insects. The next time you hear a "longbreath locust" (apparently so called be-cause it is *not* a locust and the sound is *not* made by its breath), you must not think of sound or hearing – you must think of vibrations – waves in the ether – which can be sensed by another such locust at a distance of at least eight miles. You will also have to use this theory when we return to our termite nest, or else you will be forced to think of a miracle in order to explain the communication which takes place between the outlying sections of the nest. This disposes of sound in the insect world. There are two other ways of communication which I must tell you about: Scent and Colour.

Our termites continually make use of scents, some of which we can perceive with our olfactory organ. In the Northern Transvaal there is a well-known termite known as the "stinking ant"; this emits a foul smell to a distance of three or four yards, which has the peculiar property of causing extreme nausea in most people and also in dogs. Then again all South Africans will know the characteristic smell of the common termite. This is caused by the discharge of a gas which the termite uses for other purposes. It is of the utmost importance for us in our study of termite language to make certain of what the signal of the queen really consists. After long study, I have come to the conclusion that it consists of something which would affect our senses as *scent* if it were strong enough. Things always seem pretty hopeless in the beginning when we are dealing with phenomena which lie far beyond all our senses, but "perseverance pays" must be the motto of the traveller along these dark and unknown footpaths.

Here is another reason for thinking the signal may be thought of as scent. You can easily train a pointer to track down the flying termites after they have lost their wings. He will track down a signalling queen for nearly a hundred yards against the wind; with the male he finds it difficult even over the distance of a yard.

34

But a still more important proof will take me longer to explain. The following are all the signals used by the termite:

1. The communal signal which is constantly sent out by the queen – who forms the hub of the nest. This serves to keep the community together and enables every termite to recognize every other member of the community. It is a signal which cannot be perceived by our senses.
2. The call of the workers and soldiers. This is perceived by us as sound.
3. Food messages. (Beyond our perception.) These three we will examine more closely later on.
4. Lastly, the sexual signal of the queen, which is also beyond the reach of our senses.

We know that throughout nature scent and colour are used as sexuals. If there are no brilliant colours, you may be sure there will be some scent.

Allow me to digress for a moment. I have shown you how the termite flight is the key by which the door to the sexual life is unlocked. Without flight there can be no sexual life. In the mammals the key is generally *scent*, sometimes allied to colour. This begins in the plant. The colour and perfume of flowers is of course purely a sexual phenomenon. The apes and humans have long ago lost both. But in the other mammals scent still remains as the key which makes sexual life possible – that is why it is possible to keep large mammals for years in a zoo or menagerie without the sexual passion being awakened. It is interesting to study our African kudus in relation to this fact. In the Waterberg I very often had the opportunity of watching from near at hand a wonderful spectacle. For a week or two every year the kudu cows become scented or "on heat". As soon as this passes the bulls leave the cows and segregate themselves to graze in small herds. Of course they come in contact with the cows occasionally but never evince the slightest interest. But just see what happens when the cows, in heat again, travel four or five miles to windward. A minute before all the bulls were grazing peacefully, in sleepy careless fashion. Then they get the wind. It is as if a thunderbolt has fallen in their midst. With fitful movements the beautiful heads are raised and their nostrils are snuffing the wind greedily. Their deafening bellows are heard on all sides, and immediately the whole herd, which a moment before was grazing so peacefully, is lost in a cloud of dust and we hear only the clashing of horns and bellowing of rage, because the sexual life is always preceded by the stimulation of the fighting sense. Without the special scent from the cows, their sexuality would have remained unstimulated. This can be easily proved. Take one of the smaller mammals, of a kind dependent on the sense of smell, and destroy the olfactory nerves by incision; in some cases nature does this with an ulcer. After this the male may be brought into the closest contact with the female, even in heat, but never again will he become sexually stimulated. Outside stimulation, scent or colour, is always essential to stir the sex centres. The only animals whose sex centres can be stirred without this outside stimulation are the higher apes and man. When you come to the ape and man the cultivation of scent and colour becomes fascinating and mysterious. Ask a young woman why she uses the heavenly perfumes which the chemist of our day has learnt the art of producing in such exquisite perfection. Her answer will be misleading, because she does not know the subconscious reason. It is an urge which rises from the most remote recesses of her psyche, a rudimentary and forgotten instinct from the ancient history of her race. She would be startled if she heard the true story of this urge. She would feel embarrassed if she learnt that the basis of all her perfumes were the sexual secretions of several kinds of cats, of a deer, and (the most expensive of all) the rudimentary sexual material secreted by a certain kind of whale which is now merely a pathological reminder of his life on the land millions of years ago. Musk is the universal basis of the scent sex signals in animals. Even in human beings this phenomenon may still be found. Our young woman will be astonished and perhaps a little envious, to hear that about one woman in every thousand still secretes musk on occasion. Her whole skin becomes strongly and exquisitely fragrant. As is the case with many such atavistic tendencies of our race history, this secretion of musk is found more frequently in individuals of the monkey or ape tribes. But that is the origin of the mysterious yearning which lovely perfumes awaken in the human being.

When speaking of scent you should again think of waves in the ether. It is false to assume that perfumes consist of gases or microscopic substances. Perfume itself is not entirely a physical substance. You may scent a large room for ten years with a small piece of musk and yet there will not be any loss in weight.

We appear to have gone a very long way round in order to find out of what the signal of our queen really consisted. In reality we avoided many deviations in the path which we

37

might have taken. That shows us how very patient and persevering we must be to reveal the tiniest little secret of our dear Mother Nature. Now at least we are nearly certain – never of course quite certain – that the sexual signal of the termite queen is a wave circle in the ether which in all probability would be perceived by our olfactory nerves as perfume if it could cross the threshold of perceptivity of our senses.

4

WHAT IS THE PSYCHE?

That which is known as the psyche or soul is something far beyond the reach of our senses. No one has ever seen or smelt, or heard or tasted or felt the psyche, or even a piece of it. There are two ways in which we can come on the track of the psyche. In my own innermost self I become aware of something which is not a tangible part of my physical body. This awareness of course is limited to a part of my own psyche. That of my brother is just as far beyond my direct reach as the psyche of the termite. I must accept the existence of other psyches because I am told of them. Introspection is thus one method by which I am able to affirm the existence of the psyche. But this is a separate branch of knowledge which at the moment does not concern us. Now we come to a question which will prove more interesting to us in regard to our observation of the termite. I will try again to be as little scientific and technical as possible. But I must enlarge on it and you must be patient and try to read it and understand it if you wish to grasp all the wonders of a termite nest, which will be revealed to you later on.

Remember that most of the important definitions which follow are my own and made on my own responsibility for what that may be worth. You will search scientific books in vain for confirmation of what I say. Nevertheless I flatter myself that, if you really study nature, not only will you find that all I say is true, but that it is the only key with which to unlock many dark secrets in the behaviour of living creatures.

Let us first see what science says. The psyche, so say scientific and very logical people, is a *state, of matter.* This was also their first definition of magnetism; you dare not say the psyche is something which causes a certain state of matter, for there is no proof of that. But the analogy with magnetism and later discoveries gives us a certain right to say:

First: "The psyche is something outside the reach of our senses; it causes certain states in matter, which states are within the reach of our senses."

It is of course only through movement that we can become aware of this state. Then comes the question, What is a psychological movement? Our whole life is a world of movement. We see dust and leaves blowing about in the wind; we see streams flowing and water plants swaying in them. We hear the wind and feel it; we see a little ant carrying a piece of food to its nest, we see an egg apparently unmoving, but if we have the chance of watching it long and carefully enough we see a continuous movement, which eventually results in a chicken. Which of all these movements are movements of the psyche and which are not? We need not dig too deeply into logic and metaphysics to find a definition. We will be practical and say: Only movement which has a definite motive can be a "psychological movement".

Secondly: Our own psyche is naturally the criterion which enables us to establish whether there is a motive or not.

Very logical people may not be satisfied with this part of our definition, but for the practical naturalist it is sufficient. Secondly we learn by experience that such movement occurs only in certain kinds of matter – namely organic; that it mostly originates in the organism itself, and is not dependent on forces outside itself. I purposely say *mostly* because there are many motivations in nature which are really dependent on outside forces and yet are psychological movements. There is the case of the seed of what we call the "flute" reed. Like a little powder-puff in shape the seed floats on the lightest breeze like a tiny airship, but as soon as it arrives over a pond or a marsh, the seed sinks to the ground like a bird settling on the water or damp ground. At first sight this appears to be a true psychological *motive movement* coming from within the seed, such as we very seldom find in the plant world. But on closer examination the explanation is merely this: through friction by the wind the little powder-puff, before it wrenches itself from the mother stem, receives a charge of negative electricity. The result is that all the fine hairs of the puff spring apart. As long as the hairs are spread open, the seed floats in the air; but as soon as it comes in touch with water vapour, the electricity is discharged and the puff folds up and slowly sinks to earth. By this means the plant makes certain not only that its seed shall be spread afar, but, what is of greater importance, that every seed will land on damp ground or actually in water. Here you have a number of objects which the plant achieves by utilizing natural forces outside of itself; nevertheless all these fall inside our definition as movements *with a motive* and therefore psychological.

Thirdly. Mostly – but only mostly – the movement originates in the organism itself.

The above definition will suffice for the practical naturalist. He will at times come across some puzzles, as for instance the pretended death of the *toktokkie* or the growth of a crystal; but after reflection he will find our definition still suffices.

A few words more about our classification of these motivated movements in nature and then we have finished this dry-as-dust topic and can continue with our termites. That all this has been very necessary you will see later.

I have classified it as follows:

1. Motivated movements in the plant world. These consist of four kinds:
   (*a*) Growth (for instance the turning towards the light by plants).
   (*b*) Tropism. Induced by outside influences.
   (*c*) Movements dependent on natural forces outside the organism.
   (*d*) Movements which appear to originate from within the organism, as for instance the extension of tendrils towards near objects by certain creepers; this may also be a tropism.
2. Motivated movements in the lower animal-world. The most common and most important are movements which originate in the organism itself, external forces of nature are used, but in a manner differing from that of the plants. The peculiarity of these movements is that they always follow a fixed course; the organism can never modify or change its behaviour; and this fixed behaviour is as much inherited as the organs of the body.

The investigator very soon comes to the conclusion that all motivated movements are dependent on what we call memory. These predetermined inherited motivated movements we call instinct. You come across this in all its original perfection in insects; and through the whole lower animal world you find it unchanged until you come to the apes and man and then only you find a vast and striking change in motivated movements, both in quality and in quantity.

Let us return again to the psychology of instinct. I said that the memory which constitutes this instinct is hereditary in the same way that the physical organs of the organism are hereditary. The following experiment which I myself carried out will explain what I mean.

The well-known yellow South African weaver bird, there are many kinds, but any kind may be used for this experiment, plaits a wonderful little nest at the extreme tip of a flexible branch, generally over water. You often see their nests at the end of the thin drooping twigs of the graceful weeping willow, but have you ever taken the trouble of watching to discover how the very first piece of grass is tied to the twig and what kind of knot the little bird uses? The full-grown bird is a seed eater, but the little ones are fed on worms until it is nearly time for them to leave the nest. Remember these two instinctive memories:

1. How to build the nest, and
2. How to feed the fledglings.

I hatched the eggs of the yellow weaver under canaries, for four generations. The new birds were forced to lay eggs each

43

THE SOUL OF THE WHITE ANT

time without being able to build their characteristic nest. This is the most difficult part of the experiment, but it can be done. Every time these eggs were hatched under canaries, the young ones were fed on a synthetic diet and were never allowed to see a worm or an insect. Nor did they ever see a piece of grass which might be utilized for building. Then I took this fourth generation and provided them with everything which they would need in their normal environment. Remember now that for four generations they have not seen a plaited nest or tasted a worm. From personal experience the bird cannot possibly know what to do. There can be no question of individual memory. I expected at least that there would occur *some* deviation from normal behaviour, but it was not so. When the time arrived for nesting, the birds began plaiting vigorously. They made more nests than they required. This often happens in nature as a means of protection. The eggs were hatched and the young ones were fed on worms!

This experiment shows what I mean by the inherited memory of instinct.

The second characteristic of this psyche is that the individual is incapable of deviation from a certain fixed way of behaving, in other words he cannot acquire any individual causal memory. He is bound to his inherited memories. This inherited memory is in every respect a terrible tyrant. Even when death threatens there is no escape, if escape means behaviour contrary to the inherited memory.

I will give you two examples. The black "road-maker" ants – real ants this time, not termites – are found in many parts of South Africa. They make footpaths, hundreds of yards long at times, along which they bear all kinds of plant and grass-seed to their nest. At a distance you see two streams of these ants, one apparently white, the other black. The approaching ants each carry a white seed; the retreating ants carry nothing. The ant carries the seed in its husk down into the nest. Here the husk is carefully removed. The seed is stored, and the husk is deposited outside the nest in a heap. One kind of "road-maker" ant is master of a wonderful natural secret which even man has not discovered. It knows how to prevent the germination of seed, even when this is placed in damp ground in the dark. I think they must whisper an incantation which bewitches the seed. The microscope can discover not the least flaw in such seed, yet if you pick some of the same seed and place it in exactly the same spot where the ant places his, it germinates within a few hours. But there, just see how one is led astray involuntarily when one is dealing with ants! To come back to our subject. These "road-makers" are very much afraid of water. A flood is their greatest natural enemy. Do you know why? They were originally a desert ant, more or less modern emigrants to more privileged districts, therefore they have not yet learnt how to protect their subterranean nest against long continuous rains.

Deeply rooted in them therefore is the fear of this arch-enemy of their race. The only solution they have is flight – early and as far as possible.

If you dig a little furrow across their path and fill it with water you cause the greatest bewilderment amongst the ants. On both sides of the furrow there congregates an excited throng and it takes them a very, very long while to discover that an easy solution would be to make a detour. Before they think of this, however, you place a grass stalk across the waterway to serve as a bridge and at once you will be enabled to watch very peculiar and mysterious behaviour. The ants begin to test the dangerous bridge. One by one, they try the bridge with their forelegs, stretching their bodies across it, while they cling to the bank with their back legs. They feel the bridge with their forelegs and antennae, then become aware of the water and hastily retreat to tell their companions that undoubtedly the bridge is quite unsafe. This is what happens on the bank which is on the same side as the nest, where the unladen ants congregate. On the other side of the bridge, the side farthest from the nest, the behaviour of the ants is quite different. The ants arrive here, each laden with a grass seed. Generally the seed is so heavy that the gait of the ant is very much impeded and difficult. What happens at the bridge? With apparently not the least hesitation each ant steps on to the straw with its gigantic burden. Sometimes it capsizes, but clings to the bridge with all its legs, and crosses. Always it succeeds in bringing its load to safety and hastens homewards to the nest as though nothing untoward had happened.

Here you are confronted by a riddle; the unladen ant is afraid to risk its life on the bridge; the laden ant crosses with a load which makes its passage a hundred times more dangerous. The carrying of the burden cannot lessen its awareness of the water. Now take a square piece of tin covered with earth and push it under the ants congregated on the nestward side of the bridge. When they are gathered thickly on the tin, pick this up with the ants. With a fine camel-hair brush mark as many ants as possible with a small red mark on the hinder part of the body, and then shake them on to the ground beyond the bridge. Immediately they all dash off along the path, to return shortly each carrying a grass seed, and they cross the bridge without a qualm, as if they had been crossing bridges all their lives. After a while some of your marked ants will return from the nest, having safely deposited the seed. When they come to the bridge they stop, and nothing you can do will give one single ant the courage to cross the bridge. And so you may continue from morning till night, if you have the patience of a naturalist, until almost every ant is marked with a red spot. In the end you will have learnt two things:

First, that you will never teach the ants by their own experience that the bridge can be crossed in safety. Secondly, you will never teach the ants that if the bridge is safe for a heavily laden ant it must be, proportional to the load, so much safer for an unladen ant. They prove this for themselves hundreds of times. If you were to continue this experiment for months, the ants would be able to prove this fact thousands of times, but their behaviour never changes, until at last you will give them up as hopeless. The unladen ant will never dare to cross the bridge, but as soon as he returns with his heavy burden, he crosses without hesitation.

Can you guess why the unladen ant refuses to cross and the laden ant does not? If you have investigated the psychology of animals, the behaviour of the ants will not remain a secret for very long. The behaviour of the unladen ant which leaves the nest is determined by only one instinctive urge – to fetch food. In any case it is not a very strong urge, for it always operates in opposition to the ever-present and very great urge – the *homing instinct,* the strongest of all psychological urges, except the sexual, where this is present in individuals. Higher up in the scale of animal life we call this urge "home-sickness", *heimweh*. The ants returning with the seed are drawn by two of the strongest urges:

1. Homing instinct, and
2. Bringing the food to safety.

It is as if you had tied threads to the ants and were pulling them. The thread pulling the ant away from the nest is very weak. When the ants become aware of danger and become afraid, the thread breaks. But the returning ants are drawn by two strong threads, which even a fear of death cannot break. We see therefore that the riddle was not such a very difficult one after all.

You understand now what the psychologist means when he says that the instinctive psyche cannot deviate from the inherited formula of behaviour, and that no individual can acquire a causal memory – in other words he cannot learn by his own experience.

I also said that the psyche of inherited memories is a force which cannot be turned aside even by death if escape means behaviour which conflicts with the race memory. As an example of this I will tell you about the case of the springboks on the Springbokvlakte in Waterberg. This vlakte or plain is an island of open veld in the middle of the Transvaal bushveld. The springbok is highly specialized for life on the open plain, in other words all his inherited memory is of open plains. He knows how to escape the perils which threaten him there; he knows which is the best food for him there and how he can find this; he knows when and how to change his quarters. He can see and smell over great distances. On this plain there were, twenty years ago, thousands of springboks. Now they have been exterminated. Slowly but surely people have crowded there, made farms, fenced off camps, and destroyed the springboks. To the west rose the mountains and to the north lay the endless bushveld, where they would have been absolutely safe. Death lay on the one hand and safety on the other, but they could not take the step which would have saved them. Thousands of other big game, less specialized, fled into the bush and saved themselves from extinction. Often it happened that herds of springbok were chased by hunters into the bushveld. Always they returned – sometimes the very same day – to meet death on the open plain.

There still remain two further kinds of "soul movements" or instinctive urges in nature, the classification and peculiarities of which you must know if you hope to understand even a little about the behaviour of the termite.

3. Group movements. There are some movements in individuals of a community which are determined by some purpose of benefit to the community. We term this phenomenon the "group psyche or soul". You find it in the termites, ants, baboons, apes, and in all animals which live in groups or are gregarious.

Then lastly:

4. The psyche of individual memory – that is the psyche of the primate, man and the apes, baboons and monkeys.

When you live with baboons you very soon see that the difference between the psyche of the lowest baboon and the

49

highest mammal (the dog or otter, for instance) is far greater than the difference between the psyche of the baboon and that of man.

What exactly is the difference? We know that the difference is there, but to put our meaning into words is difficult at first. A great deal of very patient work was necessary to enable me to write down in black and white of what the difference consists.

If you ask scientists what the psychological difference is between a baboon and an otter, nine out of ten will say that the baboon possesses powers of reasoning and intelligence, which the otter lacks. It would be just as clear if they said the baboon is a baboon and the otter is an otter. Neither answer takes you very far. Another scientist may say that a baboon can learn new habits more easily than an otter. This is more enlightening but does not help us a great deal.

Let us look at this race memory carefully and see what the result of it is in nature. Let us take a land bird that can fly and is very much the same in every respect as other land birds. Gradually our bird begins finding food on the beach. After millions of years he learns to catch fish in fairly deep water. As soon as this becomes a fixed habit natural selection begins to operate. The deeper the bird goes into the water, the more chance he will have of survival if he is equipped for his new life physically and psychologically. And so it goes on for another million years. The bird loses his wings, they now serve as oars; he loses his feathers, which become down; his legs become adapted for swimming – and at last we have the penguin. By the way, you will see I adhere to Darwin's theories: I never saw very much in those of De Vries. If we observe

50

the penguin or the otter, for all that I have said applies to both, we notice several important facts. If any sudden change occurs in their environment, they are completely at sea. Let me give you an example of the otter in these conditions. Once in the Waterberg during a drought which lasted for four years and when all the streams became stagnant, you would find otters all over the veld adjacent to the big waterways. There were still pools of water, but these contained no fish or crabs. The otter is a nimble creature, and you can teach him to catch birds and other small land animals in the same way as a cat does. But he cannot teach himself to do this. Hundreds of these wild otters died in the midst of plenty. At this time I managed to get hold of a pair of newly born otters. One of these I sent to Springbokvlakte, thirty miles from the nearest running water. As he was dug out of the nest shortly after birth, he had never seen a river. A bitch reared him with her own litter. He never saw or was given food other than raw meat, birds and other land animals, and he never saw water except when it was given to him in a dish to quench his thirst.

At the same time I took a newly born baboon from the mountains to the plain and reared him with a feeding-bottle. Afterwards he was fed on food which was not his natural diet. No opportunity was given him of catching or eating a living insect. When both these animals were three years old they were taken for the first time to their own natural environments, the otter to Sterk river, whence he originally came, and the baboon to the Dubbele Mountains where his mother had been shot. Both were starved for a short while previously. Here I had a wonderful opportunity of observing the great difference in behaviour of these two creatures. The otter just

51

hesitated for a moment or two, then plunged into the water, and within half an hour had caught a crab and a large carp and devoured them on the rocks.

The baboon, on the contrary, was completely lost. He was in the midst of a plenitude of natural food yet, although starving, he obviously knew nothing of turning over stones and catching the living insects which hide beneath them. There is no doubt he would have died of hunger if he had been left alone. When I turned up a stone for him, he retreated from the wriggling insects, and showed signs of fear and horror. With the greatest difficulty I succeeded in persuading him to taste a dead scorpion, from which I had removed the sting and the poison gland, and at last he was induced to catch a living one, with the result that he was immediately stung on the finger. He chose, amongst other things, to eat a wild mountain fruit which is deadly poison and his life perforce had to be saved. Such accidents never happen to wild baboons. They have learnt. Our tame baboon also eventually understood all these things, but he had to learn by painful experience.

We see then that nature has done two things for the baboon: she has given him a psyche which is able to acquire individual causal memories; and secondly she has done away with his inherited race memory. The baboon is the transition point in the animal world. He has advanced so far that in about fifty per cent, of cases there is no inherited orientation of the sexual instinct, the instinct which is the strongest inherited instinct of all. In man we find no inherited orientation of this instinct at all. Sexual desire may awaken, but the orientation must be learnt in both sexes. How has this extraordinary change in natural behaviour taken place? In the first place some great advantage must accrue to the race through the change. You will understand that on the whole the result of inherited memory is to bind a race tyrannically to a special environment. The penguin to the sea, the klip-springer to the mountains, the springbok to the plains. The more perfect race memory is, the more strictly confined will be the organism to his environment. This is the only result of natural selection. The affirmation or belief that selection and development in nature are striving after some ideal state of perfection is childish and false. In every case of highly specialized animals we find a loss of physical perfection. An exchange always takes place and the result is not perfect. When the penguin exchanged his wings for oars, he did not become more perfect; the long neck of the giraffe is a disadvantage in flight and distinctly unsightly. Nature is not a charitable institution. She is always inimical to life, or else there would be no natural selection. It is clear, too, that the race which is bound too closely to a certain environment is at a great disadvantage. If the environment suffers a sudden change, such a race is lost. It cannot change to a new environment and individuals cannot acquire new memories to enable them to cope with the changes in their environment.

In Africa it frequently happens that whole races are exterminated by such changes in nature, as for instance droughts, locust, or the arrival of other unknown enemies. To give a race the great advantage of being able to change its environment suddenly, natural selection must cause a change in the very psyche. No single or even repeated somatic change only can bring this about. There must be psychological change, too. The first and most important step is to wipe out the inherited or race memory. Unless this happens there can be no change in environment. Not only must the race memory be destroyed, but even the possibility of its being inherited must disappear from the psyche – or the change will be useless. Instead of race memory a psyche must be developed which enables every individual to acquire his own causal memory of his environment. It is this change in the baboons which has given them an advantage which every one who is familiar with them will concede.

The immediate result of this change was to make the baboon a citizen of the world. He can adapt himself to any environment – that is why we find our South African baboons in most varying surroundings. You find them on the fruitful mountains of the Cape, in the big forests and river valleys of the interior, and in the waterless deserts of the Kalahari. In every environment he acquired new habits. He learnt to catch sucking lambs and tear them open in order to drink the milk in their bellies – throughout half of South Africa. In the Northern Transvaal he has not learnt this yet. In one district of Waterberg he has learnt to place a hard fruit on a rock and break it open with a stone – his first use of an implement. Nowhere in nature will you find these things happening except in the baboons and apes.

From all this investigation we find two facts which are clear as daylight. First there is a vast psychological gulf between the psyche of the baboon and the psyche of the highest mammal below the race of primates; and secondly that the psyche of man and the psyche of the baboon are exactly the same in quality. The difference is found to be only in quantity.

In the case of the baboon we are looking at the stream near its source in the mountains. In the case of man we see the same river just before it disappears into the ocean.

Man has gone farthest in this direction, and that is the reason why he has conquered the biggest and driest deserts, the Gobi and the Sahara, the highest mountains, the deepest valleys, the tropics and the frozen Poles – and yet survived. But nature demands payment for all she gives. As we have shown there is always an exchange. The baboon and man paid an exorbitant price for their new type of psyche – a price which is bound surely but slowly to bring about their natural extermination. One day, when I have finished telling you about the termites, I may tell you why I think that.

Only one more word about the psyche of individual causal memory. The old animal psyche of race memory does not actually get destroyed, but it is paralysed by a kind of permanent inhibition. But it still remains and can be artificially stimulated into function. This, I think, is the greatest discovery I made during an observation of the wild baboon lasting over three years. There is not the least doubt to my mind that the so-called subconscious psyche of man is not a wonderful creation of natural selection which leads to ideal perfection, but is in fact only the old animal psyche in a state of inhibition; and which in abnormal circumstances is released and leads to serious psychological disorders.

We have gone a tremendous detour, but now at last we have reached the point where, with a clear conscience, we can investigate the communal psyche of the termite.

5

LUMINOSITY IN THE ANIMAL KINGDOM

The ordinary use of light by the glow-worm and firefly is well known to dwellers in South Africa. Here in the Transvaal the fireflies at times make an amazing show. On the slopes of the Highveld they appear at times in such numbers that the river-beds stretch into the night like streams of light as far as the eye can see. I must confess at once that I do not know for certain what is the motive of this signal. In spite of long and careful observation, I never succeeded in actually seeing the result, if there was one, of the signal. It almost seems as though the insect purposely hides her motive when she becomes aware of being observed. In this respect the firefly reminds me of the pollination of one of our grasses, *Aristida*. If you ever wish to undertake a heartbreaking and hopeless investigation, I advise you to try to be a witness to this pollination. I remember how I watched one whole day until after midnight at the side of the unpollinated plant. At night acetylene mine lamps were lit which cast a circle of light as clear as day for nearly a hundred yards round the plant. And then at last, when weary and exhausted I went to sleep for a couple of hours, I woke to find that the miracle had taken place while I slept – for the pollination takes place when you least expect it: an hour or two before daybreak. In the same way I spent many sleepless nights watching the firefly and never convinced myself what the motive of the signal could be. I think it is a sexual signal. If there is a doubt, it arises through the fact that the sexes are not dependent only on the light for their sexual life. There are other land creatures which also become luminous periodically. The most wonderful, certainly the most entrancing, is the large green centipede which is found in tropical parts of Africa. Perhaps this gigantic centipede causes more fear and horror in people unused to handling such creatures than any other. For some reason – which I do not know – this monster sometimes becomes luminous. It is a rare occurrence. I have only seen it twice. The spectacle is one which the lucky beholder will never forget. If you come across the creature in the dark, while it is luminous, your first conclusion is that it must be a necklace of precious jewels. What would not a lovely lady give for a necklace like that! It is about twelve inches long – both mine were females – and while the luminosity lasts the creature, usually so nimble and quick, appears to be in a state of cataleptic paralysis. It appears as though all its energy is being used for the generation of the brilliant light. So bright is the illumination that line print can easily be read in a dark room at a distance of two feet. What causes the light? I have no idea. A friend of mine, a chemist, examined all the organs of one of these luminous centipedes and he could find no trace of any known light-giving element; under the low power of the microscope the light appeared to come from two luminous patches near the ends of each segment of the body. The light is in continuous movement, an irregular glowing and paling which expands and contracts in concentric circles coming from an intense centre of white light. The circles of light are independent of each other. Coincident with the change in intensity there is a constant and amazing change in the colours of the circles of light. Passing outwards from the white centre, the colours appear in the following order: light yellow, light green, emerald green, dark green, blue, dark blue, red, purple, violet. The source of the light lies within the body of the insect and is irradiated through the skin. In the glow-worm the source of the light appears to be outside the skin. You will see that there is a great unexplored field of work in connection with the signals of animals. That is why I have told you about luminosity to complete our list of signals. I like writing about the firefly, too, for the very reason that this little insect is still wrapped in intriguing mystery.

What is the motive of the light? What *is* the light? I must confess ignorance. I can tell you very well what it is *not,* but the opposite side of the balance sheet will remain blank. This happens frequently when we study animals which make use of well-known forces of nature.

The South African jelly-fish, for example, has as a means of defence a charge of electricity, with which he shocks you if he touches you under the water. Now the whole of the body of the jelly-fish is filled with water, which is a perfect conductor without insulation; it is surrounded by seawater which is a far better conductor than the human body. In such conditions it appears impossible for the creature to generate a charge of electricity and still more impossible to direct it through human skin. The creature simply *cannot* do it – yet it does!

While we are talking of fireflies and glow-worms, I want to

question one theory – very diffidently. The famous Fabre died under the firm impression that he had discovered the secret of the light. On the skin of the insect we find a white powder, which looks very much like frost. On to this the insect projects two streams of air; the light disappears in the absence of oxygen. Fabre therefore concluded that the phenomenon was nothing else than oxidation. He had no further doubts and his statement has been repeated by many writers. I would like to say this: If it *is* oxidation, then it is a form of oxidation which is found nowhere else in nature, which the cleverest chemist cannot imitate, and which would necessitate a complete revision of all our beliefs about the properties of oxygen.

Oxidation always generates heat. If it takes place very slowly – like for instance the rusting of a metal – then the heat is generated so slowly that it is not noticed – but still there is heat. If oxidation takes place rapidly, the generation of heat becomes explosive. When oxidation takes place quickly enough to cause light, there *must* be a previous and continuous generation of heat. Oxidation without this phenomenon is just as impossible as fire without light or heat. If oxygen is necessary for the firefly's light, that does not prove that the light is due to oxidation, as Fabre claimed. Take several fireflies and test them with a sensitive thermometer; you will find there is no rise of temperature due to the light. One could prove that to produce a light equal in strength to that of the firefly for one hour, the bodies of more than eighteen hundred fireflies would have to be burnt. I think Fabre's theory was wrong.

Another word about light. Some years ago a Japanese naturalist discovered that the firefly emits rays which affect a photographic plate *through* the black covering. These rays must be those which are imperceptible to the human eye. I have been unable to test this myself, or to discover whether our fireflies also emit these rays.

6

THE COMPOSITE ANIMAL

The division "group soul" in our classification of psychological movements is one which the human mind finds most difficult to understand. The further we depart from our own psychological characteristics, the more mystified and puzzled do we become, and the true group soul is the opposite extreme to the psyche, i.e. of the primate, which consists of uninherited, individual causal memory of the environment. The most perfect example of the group soul can be observed in our own bodies. The human body is composed of a number of organs, each connected by a visible or invisible thread to the central point, the brain. Each organ is in constant activity and has a separate purpose – at least the purpose appears to be separate and independent; but on closer observation we find that all the organs are really working for a communal purpose. The influence dominating all the organs comes from one central point. In no single organ can we find a real independent purpose. After the composite physical body of a highly developed animal like man, there is no better example of the functioning of a group soul than the termitary.

I am now entering a province which will tax your credulity to the utmost, so I will go slowly step by step, making certain of one before we take the next. I promise that I will make no statement which cannot be proved experimentally and, when the facts appear too wonderful and incredible, I will tell you the experiments in order to enable you to repeat them and perhaps even improve on them.

In everyone who carefully observes the termite, the question is bound to arise, "Why do they continue working? What is the mainspring of this restless activity?" Restless it is indeed. Do you know that of equally developed creatures the termite is the only one which apparently never rests or sleeps? However carefully you observe it, you will never surprise the termite at rest or asleep.

What is the aim of this ceaseless toil and struggle? In other individual animals nature has planted great irresistible urges, the sexual and parental urge, the urge to defence, the urge for food and drink. These urges constitute the psyche of the individual and dominate its movements. In the individual termite there are none of these urges to act as a driving force.

The answers to these questions really constitute the definition of a true group soul. In order to be perfectly clear I will give my line of investigation in the form of theses.

1. All the movements of the termite are controlled from without the individual. The termite possesses no vestige of free will, or power of choice. The only quality it possesses is automobility – power of moving itself. It puts itself into motion, but when this motion will take place or what will be done with it, is decided, controlled from without. Circumstances may render the termite's work useless and vain; in cases where the simplest insect individually controlled

would shrink from its destiny the termite must carry on. It must follow the path along which the unseen arbiter of its fate urges it to go.

2. The whole behaviour of the termite is determined from without by an influence – we may call it a thread by which he is firmly tied to the queen's cell. This invisible influence streams from the organism of the queen alone. It is a power beyond our senses; it can penetrate all material barriers, even such as thin steel or iron plates.

3. Distance lessens the influence: it has power only between fixed limits.

4. The somatic death of the queen destroys the influence immediately. Injuries and wounds sustained by the queen weaken the influence in proportion to the size of the injury.

5. The termitary is a separate composite animal at a certain stage of development, and lack of automobility alone differentiates it from other such animals.

6. The termite has descended from an ordinary flying solitary insect. The development of specialized groups and their amalgamation is a late occurrence in the race-history of the termite.

7. The termitary is an example of the method in which composite and highly developed animals like the mammals came into being.

8. The body of a mammal with its many vital organs can be looked upon as a community with specialized individuals grouped into organs, the whole community forming the composite animal. The higher the development of the animal, the higher the specialization of the groups.

9. This phenomenon of specialized groups of individuals being

developed into different organs and becoming a composite animal can actually be observed to-day in nature.

The group soul, which is surely the most amazing psychological phenomenon in the natural world and gives the strongest proof that it may be possible for a psychological influence to have effect on an organism at a distance, is the result of this communal life. It is important therefore that we should observe the composite organism and try to understand it. The particular kind of termite on which I based these observations is one of the most common, in South Africa, and everyone will be able to study it.

If you make a breach in any termite's nest on the veld, it will in all likelihood be the nest of the kind of which I am speaking. In the breach you will see two kinds of insects, differing so greatly from each other that if you know nothing of termites it will take a great deal to convince you that they had the same mother and father. One is an ordinary whitish insect with strong jaws, and two black spots which appear to be eyes. The other, under a magnifying glass, looks like a nightmarish monster. It is reddish yellow in colour but when many are massed together the red colour becomes dominant. The body ends in a massive triangular head tapering to a long black hornlike needle or syringe. Below the neck there are four almost rudimentary legs in addition to the other ordinary functioning legs. This needle or syringe is in direct communication with a large reservoir of fluid. In your wildest imagination you could not create a creature more totally cut off from the outside world. Except its two antennae, there is no trace or sign of any organ of sense. How and what the creature eats is a riddle. The only possible food would have to be a thin fluid. The ordinary food which is carried into the nest must have undergone a great change in the bodies of the other termites before this horned beast could make use of it. It is not necessary for our purpose to theorize about all the probable functions of these insects. With a fairly powerful magnifying glass you will see at once that the behaviour of these two kinds of termites in the breach is not identical. The syringe-bearers throng in increasing numbers and, with their syringes pointing outwards, quickly form a ring round the opening. If you tease one of these termites with a stiff bristle, a kind of conclusive movement passes over it, while it makes a stabbing movement with its weapon in all directions. Eventually a crystal clear drop of sticky fluid appears at the end of the syringe. This fluid contains a certain amount of stinging acid. There can be no doubt that these syringe-bearers are there to defend the nest against the enemy, relying on their terrifying appearance as well as their weapons. Apart from this they do nothing. Protected by this cordon of defenders, the other termites begin working busily. They begin to mend the breach, or to heal the wound. From the depths of the termitary, each appears carrying a tiny grain of sand or earth in its jaws. With the help of similar rudimentary legs as those described in the syringe-bearers, the grain is turned about rapidly. Under the microscope you will find that the object of this is to coat it with a similar sticky fluid. It is then fastened to some section of the wound. It cannot fall. If you touch the newly built section, your fingers become sticky, as if you had touched some syrup. This fluid has the property of evaporating very rapidly, and as soon as evaporation has taken place the stickiness disappears.

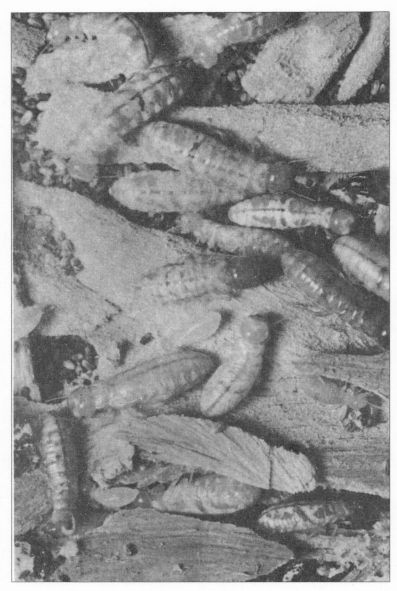

A group of termites in which can be seen workers, soldiers and nymphs.

Termitary material.

One of my theses was that the termitary is a separate and perfect animal, which lacks only the power of moving from place to place. I will give you my proofs of this little by little, and the explanation will make clear at the same time the beginning and development of the group soul. Up to now you have learnt what happens in a wounded termitary. Let us turn our attention for a moment to a far more developed composite organism before we return to the termitary.

I take for granted that you have a general idea of the construction of your own body and how that machine works. You know that your body consists of millions of cells, through which there is constantly flowing a fluid which we term blood.

67

Termitary material.

The fluid consists chiefly of two separate kinds of organism, red and white corpuscles, each of which is a living cell having a life or soul of its own as well as a group soul. These corpuscles build up the body, mend wounds and attack germs. Metchnikoff's conclusions in this connection, although doubtful in certain respects, are nevertheless true in their general lines.

The attacking microbes are themselves attacked and devoured in the wound or in the natural orifices, or, if they succeed in entering, the fight is carried on in the cells and passages. Every wound swarms with defending white corpuscles. If a germ of disease enters the system there is an even leuco-

cytosis or increase of white corpuscles. Both growth and healing always take place from within outwards. Covering the
vital organs we have the epidermis or skin, a tough impenetrable covering which shuts out light and air. The corpuscles
of the blood are afraid of air and light. The growth of the body
is more wonderful and mysterious than we realize. We are far
too prone to consider every ordinary natural phenomenon as
a kind of axiom which needs no explanation, like, for instance, the fall of an apple to the ground. Just consider for a
moment the growth of the body, with particular reference to
the skin. Growth always takes place from within outward. But
we do not find a piece of skin being removed, a piece of an
organ being built, and then a new skin being grown over the
wound. The growth takes place under the skin. You would be
justified in expecting either that the skin should stretch or
that a new piece of the body should be grown on top of the
old skin and then a new skin over that, so that if you cut into
the body you would find layers of old skin. Neither of these
things happen. Well, you say, of course the skin grows in the
same way that the internal parts grow. It is easy to say this, but
we cannot find any proof of it. We know that all growth is
caused by the corpuscles in the blood-stream. But we know
that these corpuscles never come in contact with the dermis
or outer skin. How this outer skin grows at the same rate as
the other organs we cannot explain. You know, too, that your
body consists of several large organs, each of which functions
independently. According to our classification each of these is a
separate animal with a separate psyche. Then you have another
organ which is the home of the group soul – the brain – the
centre of the community which is the body.

69

You have learnt by this time that soul and life are identical. Every definition for soul will be equally as good for *life,* and vice versa. I have never observed any occurrence which tended to prove that soul and life were two separate entities. They are one and the same. The only difference lies in the two names, which have been given to the same thing.

A small injury to the central point, the brain, is sufficient to cause immediate death of the whole body. The growth and life of the body can continue only with the help of the red and white corpuscles of the blood. Food is taken through a foramen, the mouth, and, after being changed or digested by certain organs, is absorbed by the corpuscles. Ninety per cent of this food is carried to different parts of the body and used as cells to make new muscle, sinews and bone. A portion of the food consists of unassimilable material, but this must be absorbed by the corpuscles with that which is assimilable, because it forms part of the assimilable material. Within their own bodies, the corpuscles separate the assimilable and unassimilable, and the waste is eventually cast from the body as excreta.

I have just said that a small injury of the brain is sufficient to cause the death of the body. Let us study some of the peculiar and mysterious aspects of the condition we call death.

We know that a living person can remain in water for ten days without any part of his skin dissolving. The channel swimmers stay in the sea for twenty-four hours and their skin is quite undamaged by this immersion. Water cannot wash away any part of the living skin, in fact the skin of a living man is as insoluble in water as india-rubber. The whole body of a living person is full of elasticity and possesses a great power of resistance to blows of blunt objects. Remember these two characteristics:

1. Insolubility of the skin.
2. The general touch-resisting powers and the elasticity of the whole living body.

The change which takes place in these two respects after death is astounding. Have you ever seen a drowned man who has been in the water for some hours? You will remember the gruesome change. What has caused this? As soon as life ends, the epidermis becomes more and more soluble in water; and the body immediately begins to lose its elasticity and power of resistance, until at last even a child could poke a blunt object right through the body. To put it baldly, every part becomes spongy and falls into decay. The physiologist expresses all this differently, generally in long Latin or Greek words, but the meaning remains unchanged. He says: As soon as death has taken place, the more complex components break up into simpler ones. Microbes appear, to hasten the process. This does not help us to understand things more clearly, for the following reasons:

The body consists largely of dead matter. All the cell walls and the outer skin are made up of ordinary dead matter – or chemical substances. What do the corpuscles do to prevent the solubility of the skin and to protect the elasticity and structure of the body? No one knows. The presence or absence of the corpuscles makes this vast difference. You have heard doubtless of a certain mysterious phenomenon in chemistry – how the mere presence of one element can change the chemical make-up of another element. The same kind of function is played by the living corpuscles in the bloodstream. This secret, inexplicable influence, which their mere presence has on the chemical and physical character of dead matter, is the mystery of life. In the simplest living cell, such as the blood corpuscle, we find something which not only enables it to move, but which also prevents the breaking up of the cell material. Antagonistic forces of nature are always present ready to break up the cell. Here we find the beginning of the struggle for life – the attempt to frustrate the inimical forces of nature. The first purpose or urge is a tug of war between the life or soul and matter. This influence at a distance of certain substances specially secreted by the body for this purpose is a well-known biological phenomenon.

The human body possesses a number of ductless glands, whose function it is to produce certain secretions. The mere presence of these secretions exercises a great influence on the whole physical make-up. The adrenal glands for instance produce a substance, adrenaline, which is responsible, amongst other things, for the blood pressure. The gland itself is completely isolated from the rest of the body and yet has this influence at a distance.

After this lesson in physiology and biology, we can now return to study the termitary in the light of our new knowledge. You may wonder how I can call a heap of dead earth like the termitary a living animal. Do not forget that the termitary is no more dead than the dead matter of cell walls which constitutes nine-tenths of your own body. We are ourselves no more than dead termitaries, through which circulates a living substance.

If you destroy a termitary you find firstly a tough resistant skin all around it. Under this skin you find that the whole termitary consists of cells through which a living stream constantly circulates. As you go deeper you find large passages and eventually a hollow, partly or entirely filled with more cells, which are of a different consistency from those of the actual heap. These cells no longer consist of earth and are covered within and without with a kind of mould. This mould is often used in South Africa to make yeast. If you go deep enough and observe carefully you will find at the very bottom a passage which goes right into the earth. If the termitary is an old one and placed on top of a dry kopje or hill, this passage descends to an incredible depth. It is the canal by which the termites get their water supply. They continue the shaft until at last they reach permanently moist ground. On the farm Rietfontein in Waterberg I had the opportunity of following such a passage to a depth of more than 57 feet through earth as hard as rock in the side of a mine pit. The termites need a great deal of moisture. More than ninety per cent of their tiny bodies consists of water, and the whole termitary is always damp and filled with water vapour. Where they managed to get all this moisture in our dry districts would have remained a dark secret if someone had not discovered the existence of the deep vertical aqueduct.

7

SOMATIC DEATH

In an earlier chapter I drew attention to some of the effects on the human body of somatic death.

The final result may be expressed as follows: The chemical constituents of the cell walls of organic material are very unstable. In ordinary circumstances they tend to break down into simpler elements, or else new and more stable combinations take place. The final result is that organic matter as such disappears. The coherence of these unstable constituents is maintained by the mere presence of living moving matter in the vicinity of the cell walls. I used the example, for a special purpose, of the common phenomenon which occurs after death, the solubility of the human skin in water, and I emphasized the fact that although the living elements in the bloodstream, which heal the skin and keep it healthy, do not actually come into contact with the outer skin, yet their mere presence in the vicinity is sufficient to maintain the stability of the unstable components. In other words, the presence of these living elements safeguards the skin against its ever-present tendency towards dissolution. This is the first function of what we call life or soul.

One can always tell by superficial examination whether a

termitary is alive or dead. In general the process of dissolution is not only analogous to the dissolution which takes place in the human body, but it is also similar. We find exactly the same appearance of undisguised lifelessness; there is the same change in smell, not the same smell, ascribable to the same causes, namely the dissolution of chemical constituents; there is the same immediate loss of the defensive toughness of the skin. The innermost cell-structure falls to pieces, only dust and ashes remain.

The similarity of the two phenomena becomes even more convincing if you examine the termitary in detail. Look at the skin. The covering layer of an old termitary in dry seasons is thick and impenetrable, hard as cement. After long rain it becomes softer, in the same way that human skin becomes softer after long immersion in water. The living stream of termites constantly circulating through the termitary never comes into contact with the outer skin. The termites never renew the skin from the outside. Sometimes you see patches of renewal. The growth or healing, as the case may be, always occurs from within outwards, as in the human skin. But the construction of new patches is a peculiar phenomenon, with a particular purpose. As far as the skin is concerned in an old full-grown termitary, you will never observe the termites doing anything to keep it in condition. Such an old termitary is exposed year after year to torrents of rain, terrible droughts, scorching heat, frost, hail and wind, yet the skin remains undamaged. In cases of actual trauma, through hail for instance, healing takes place by the functioning of the two little creatures in the blood-stream – I mean the two kinds of termite. The living skin in general appears to be insoluble in water. Even during continuous rain you will not find the least portion of the living skin washed away. I am speaking generally, as of course we do occasionally find exceptions to every rule. For instance, we sometimes find various forms of abnormal growth, real diseases which expose the whole structure to danger. The termites are in these cases just as stupid as the blood-stream in a human may be. Sometimes the reason is obvious. You can encourage abnormal growth artificially by stimulation and other influences both in the human and in the termitary. A common abnormality is the growth of a long narrow tower which is constantly destroyed by wind and bad weather. This is an abnormal deviation from the usual pointed summit, which is found on termitaries amongst trees. The base of the tower is often so small that it is impossible for it to carry the superstructure. Yet every time the tower falls over it is built up anew. This is not only great waste of energy, but the abnormality often becomes a danger to the whole community.

What constitutes the difference in quality between the skin of a dead termitary and that of a living one? What keeps the outer layer whole and healthy as long as the living stream continues moving within? What causes the cell walls to retain their structure intact, and what causes them to fall apart as soon as the termites die? There appears to be only one theory which conforms to modern scientific knowledge: there must be some kind of power projected from the living stream which influences the chemical constituents of organic bodies. This functions in the termitary as in the human body.

I am trying my utmost to prove that the termitary must be looked upon, not as a heap of dead earth, but as a separate animal at a certain stage of development. You must take my word for it that all this is very important and necessary if we are to get even a faint inkling of the perfect group soul and its characteristics. To be sure that we are quite clear in our minds, let us tabulate the similarities between our own physical body and the termitary:

1. We have just seen that both possess some mysterious power which exercises an influence on the whole structure and is the cause of its stability.

2. Both the human body and the termitary consist of a structure of cells covered with a thick skin. An inhabitant of Mars who had learnt enough of our earth to divide matter into organic and inorganic would not hesitate for one moment to clasify a piece of termitary as organic. The only difference would be that, for a piece of human body, he would need a microscope to study the structure, whereas in a termitary he could see it with the naked eye.

3. Moving through the cell structure under the skin we find a living stream consisting of two kinds of organisms which both in man and the termite have the same functions. The white blood corpuscles quickly form a defensive circle round a wound. They are there for apparently one purpose only, to prevent the invasion of strange hostile organisms. The other, or red, blood corpuscles busy themselves with repairing the injury. From the innermost part of the body these latter bear material for new cells which eventually are covered with new skin.

   If you make a wound in a termitary, the living stream is seen at once. The red syringe bearers form a circle of defence round the wound. Their only function is to prevent the entry of enemies by their fearful appearance or by actual defence. For purposes of defence they secrete a clear, sticky, stinging acid. The other termites of the living stream at once begin repairing the wound. They carry material from the depths of the termitary to build up the new cell structure, which eventually is covered with new skin.

4. The human body takes food through a foramen – the mouth. The food is carried to certain organs where it undergoes a chemical change; afterwards it is taken up by the blood-stream and utilized by the red corpuscles for building purposes.

   In the termitary, food is taken through several foramina and roughly masticated. It is then carried to different centres, where a certain kind of termite transforms it chemically; it then enters the living stream and is used as food for the different members of the community and for building purposes. With a magnifying glass you can observe how each termite uses a drop of fluid from his own body to cover each minute grain which is used for building. This fluid holds the structure together. Most of the water used is carried up the vertical shaft leading from subterranean sources of moisture.

I wish to digress here in order to discuss normal and abnormal growth from another angle.

Physical growth is the most perfect example in nature of the psyche of inherited memory. It always appears very wonderful and inexplicable. We humans use our own consciousness as a criterion for classification. Eventually we discover that this consciousness can never be a criterion for psychological processes different from our own. We are inclined, for instance, to be amazed at the abnormal functioning of the subconscious mind. When we discover, however, that the subconscious mind is no more than the rudimentary animal psyche still present in man, and that all the wonders which abnormal functioning bring forth are merely usual everyday occurrences in lower animals, we need be less mystified. In the same way we are amazed at our own physical growth. But when we study similar phenomena in nature; when we begin classifying our knowledge, we are forced to surrender our false criterion. We tend to believe that the psyche which directs human growth is something far beyond our own comprehension. This power we think does miracles which we could not do, and it appears to have some purpose far beyond our own understanding. Then, however, we begin to discover that the psyche which directs physical growth is in some respects more stupid and more ignorant than the psyche of a child. Even the "roadmaker" ant which we observed a short while ago, which would take years to learn that twice two always makes four, is a genius compared to this psyche. The psyche of physical growth comes lowest in the scale when "Learn by experience" is our rule of measure. If you take reasoning powers as your measure, this psyche comes even lower.

Of course when you realize that the same psyche which will from its own experience never learn that two and two make four, can, beginning with a single cell, build up an elephant or a person, or an oak tree cell by cell, then you begin getting a little muddled. That is because you use different measures.

If you were to discover that in every elephant, every

human, every oak tree, there were parts which were built wrongly in a most stupid fashion; if you were to find elephants with five legs, with deformed jaws, with regular but abnormal cell structures which form a danger to the whole body; if you were to discover that abnormal growth is often persevered in, in spite of constant destruction through the inherent weakness of structure – just as we saw in the termites with their little tower – then you would become aware of the fact that one measure cannot be used for classification.

You will come to another important conclusion. Every psychologist who studies the group soul in nature seeks an answer to the question: Is there some powerful group soul above and beyond nature which dominates all natural phenomena and directs them to some goal? It appears a hopeless task to seek an answer in nature. Every truthful naturalist, who is not led astray by his own hopes and longings, will always doubt his ability to give a truthful answer. It is possible that we see only a small arc of a gigantic circle, that the means and ways of the universal soul lie far beyond our human understanding.

It is often said that the purpose of life is natural development, it being taken for granted that the development of living creatures leads to a state of absolute perfection, not relative perfection. All that development does, however, is to equip the organism to withstand the enemies that assail it in a special environment. For every new weapon it receives, it must lay down an old one. Man who has developed the furthest psychologically, has paid the dearest for his psyche of individual causal memory. We have seen that the psyche which directs growth possesses no vestige of the powers of learning by experience, of reasoning, of intelligence, as we call it. When we make our own deepest feelings the arbiter, we are dismayed. For we seek in vain in nature for love, sympathy, pity, justice, altruism, protection of the innocent and weak. From the very beginnings of life we hear a chorus of anguish. Pain is a condition of existence. Escape from pain is the purpose in all striving.

And Nature? Pitiless cruelty, torment, and destruction of the weak and innocent. The thief, the assassin, the blood-stained robber, these are her favourites, these are the psychological types which are the triumphant victors of the strife.

The psyche, which we see faint and barely recognizable in the higher mammals, attaining its highest pinnacle in man, seems to be an exception to the great principles which dominate the universe. So the hope arises there is some purpose in nature, whose guiding principle is a psyche similar but infinitely more developed than the soul of the primate. If this is so, we seek in vain for evidence in our natural surroundings. We are as little able to comprehend such an exalted psyche as the termite can comprehend man, who orders his own aims and purposes throughout life.

If Nature possesses a universal psyche, it is one far above the common and most impelling feelings of the human psyche. She certainly has never wept in sympathy, nor stretched a hand protectively over even the most beautiful or innocent of her creatures.

8

THE DEVELOPMENT OF THE COMPOSITE ANIMAL

I have taken great pains to prove that the termitary is a separate and composite animal in exactly the same way that man is a separate composite animal. Only the power of locomotion is absent. We must not forget, however, that there are other animals who have not the power of movement.

All this may remind you of the mountain in labour, which eventually produced a very small mouse. The facts I have given, however, are as strictly true as any other established biological phenomenon, and it is necessary to accept them if you wish to understand the life history of the termite.

If you make a wound in the round termitary made by *Eutermes*, later called *Trinervitermes* – a small round vertical hole with a walking stick, for instance, and then isolate the wound with a sharp circular cut through the skin, the termites begin as usual to repair the wound. But what you have done causes in many cases a curious reflex. The termites begin abnormal building. Instead of repairing the cells and passages and growing a new skin over this, they build a tower. I believe the stimulus is the entry of sunlight. If the base is too small, the tower topples over again and again as soon as it reaches a certain height, and just as often the termites reconstruct it.

The tower is not only unnecessary to the termitary, but actually a disadvantage.

It is a disturbing influence which throws the normal course of life of the organism into disorder. It is analogous to the growth of a cancer.

Catch a pair of our common house lizards and tame them. With a lancet make two or three longitudinal cuts in the tail. In some cases you will initiate a curious reflex and an abnormal growth will begin. Instead of merely repairing the wound, a new tail is grown. If you amputate the new tail, you may find a double tail sprouting. In this way you can – if all goes well – manufacture a lizard with seven tails. In the same way we can manufacture a termitary with seven towers, to the great disadvantage of the whole community. We cannot make a lizard's tail; nor can we make a tower with the same materials and in the same way as the termite. But we would be far too clever to build in such a faulty, unnecessary fashion.

I will not try to bring any further proofs of the similarity between the termitary and other animals, but if this theory is borne in mind, constant proof will be forthcoming when the termite is studied. The insects themselves should always be thought of as the blood-stream and organs of a single animal.

If the highly developed, highly specialized animals originally developed from communities like the termite, one should be able to find instances of such symbiosis, which is more than mere partnership, low down in the scale of organic life. There are many such instances, which justify us in believing that organisms of several kinds can result in a successful amalgamation. Of this nature is the union between fungus and alga to form a lichen, which differs enormously from both original

83

ones. But the object and actual results of the process are much more clearly seen when we meet it fairly high in the animal kingdom. In the sea around the African coast there can be found a hundred kinds of a certain species of marine creature. Its scientific name is *Hydromedusa,* and there is a related species known as *Siphonophora.* We will observe *Siphonophora.* There is no other animal of its size in the ocean which can boast of so large a bibliography. Ernst Hackel and other famous naturalists spent years studying, describing and classifying them. The great peculiarity of these creatures is that every full-grown specimen is a composite animal composed of hundreds of individuals. The single individual is born by a budding process from the generative group of the composite animal. These newly born individuals swim round freely and are able to continue life singly and reproduce themselves. Each is a perfect marine creature with mouth, stomach, swimming apparatus and sexual organs. If by chance a group of *Siphonophora* happens to meet, they cling to each other. In some species organic union takes place immediately, in others something less than this. But apart from this small difference the final result is the same. Immediately after the union the single individuals undergo a curious change. One group forms a complicated swimming apparatus; another group becomes the stomach and digestive system; and yet another group develops into the sexual organs of the composite animal. One group even takes on hepatic functions and becomes the liver. Each individual of such a group loses all its separate organic functions. Those of the stomach group, for instance, forget they ever sought food or had a sexual life of their own. The new organism is a perfect whole animal. Were you to see it in its perfect

84

stage you would not dream that it had been formed in this way from separate individuals. Yet one can break it up again! One can tear apart each individual until the whole animal has been disorganized. One might suppose death would be the result, but not at all. Each little part begins to stir in the water. Slowly it repairs its lost organs and functions until at last it once again is a perfect individual, as different from the composite *Siphonophora* as the camel from the whale.

One can repeat this process innumerable times without apparently injuring either the individual or the composite creature.

In such a way our termitary has been formed; in the same way the individuals have undergone wonderful changes in order to form group organs. In every termitary there is a brain, a stomach, a liver and sexual organs which ensure the propagation of the race. They have legs and arms for gathering food; they have a mouth. If natural selection continues to operate, the final result may be a termitary which moves slowly over the veld. There are hundreds of facts, biological and psychological, in nature which prove all highly developed animals have been formed from separate organisms. Once I collected all the facts and classified them, hoping to startle the scientific world. Unfortunately my tower collapsed, not because it was wrongly built, but because other naturalists had already become aware of all this. Claude Bernard in his opening address to the French Academy (1869), Dr. Durand de Gos, in his *Electrodynamique Vitale* (1855) and *Variétés Philosophiques* (1857), tried to show that the vital organs of man were separate animals.

In our own time Jean Finot in his optimistic demonstration

on Life and Death wrote: "The teaching that the human organism is composed of separate animals, each with a separate nervous system, will, we hope, find more and more proof in the scientific investigation of our time."

Another fact one should constantly remember is that, if there is the least grain of truth in this theory of development, then just as certainly the termite was originally a perfect flying individual insect, of which the queen and king are the prototypes. The union of these individuals and the wonderful changes which resulted from it is a late development in the history of the race. If the blind, wingless, sexless soldiers and workers are not a degeneration of the perfect king and queen type, then the opposite conclusion will have to be accepted: the perfect king and queen must be a development from one or other of the sexless types, and that cannot be the case. There are other biological facts which indicate that the imperfect types are the result of degenerative change of the perfect insect. The rudiments of wing buds and of sexual organs in the sexless types show clearly the way development, or rather degeneration, has gone.

9

THE BIRTH OF THE
TERMITE COMMUNITY

U p to the present we have observed the termites and the termitary from without. We will now study the termitary and the growth and life history of the termites from within the nest. Every step will prove a surprise; we will see many things which appear incredible. The termite differs in every respect from all other insects. Morphologically there is little in nature which reminds us of the termite. Their onto-logical development is a constant surprise; phylogenetically one must look in the ocean for an analogous circle of development. The entomologist who made the acquaintance of the termite for the first time, would be justified in thinking it to be an immigrant from a different planet.

To mention one thing only – the wings. Where can one find in nature an organism which during its own lifetime will yield up the mightiest of all weapons in the struggle for life – its wings? This abandonment of wings is an example of the surprises with which the termite constantly provides us.

I give some illustrations of the different inmates of a Trans-vaal termitary. One can scarcely believe that they are the chil-dren of one father and mother. We have seen how the kings and queens leave the nests in swarms; how they *must* fly to unlock their sexual life; how the queen sends a signal; how both sexes discard their wings as soon as they reach the ground after their one and only flight. The development of the wings is very interesting. In the sexual type one can see the wing-buds quite early in life. When the insect has shed its skin for the last time and is full-grown, the wings begin to grow from these buds with a kind of hinge which allows for the greatest possible range of movement. It is from this hinge that the insect breaks its wings with a lightning-like movement. She takes hold of the wing-buds with the nearest pair of legs, which appear to be specially adapted for this purpose, shifts them along the bud until they reach the hinge, and detaches the wings.

When they have been shed, one can find no wound to indicate the spot of attachment, as one might expect. There must be some organic union, there must be some attachment to the central system which enables the wings to be set into motion. But there is no sign of this immediately after the wings are detached. How so complicated an organ, which is so powerful and which is under complete control of the insect, can give so little evidence of organic union with the body remains a mystery. One moment the insect is flying, a moment later the wings are detached, yet one finds no evidence of a lesion.

Another point of interest. The insect appears to be able to discard the wings by a voluntary movement of the wing itself. Before flight has taken place, she will struggle to free herself if she is held by the wings, without the wings becoming detached. If, however, she has experienced the sensation of flight, even *one* movement of the wings appears to be sufficient to

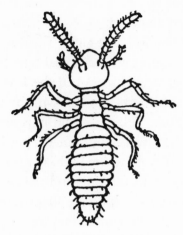

(*Trinervitermes* magnified.) Etiolated, newly hatched termite. *Colour:*White. All classes and both sexes are found. Sex organs rudimentary, disappearing as development proceeds. Entirely blind. In some individuals rudimentary pigmented spots are found in place of eyes. These, too, disappear. In others, rudimentary wing buds appear, which never develop.

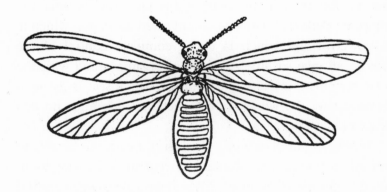

(*Trinervitermes* magnified.) King and queen at time of flight. Perfect insects with fully developed eyes, wings and sex organs. *Colour*: Dark brown, with red markings. Highly pigmented. *Functions*: 1. Reproduction. 2. Analogous to motor and sensory centres of brain in higher animals.

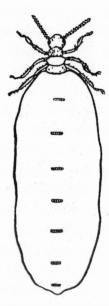

(*Bellicosus* magnified.) Queen. Beginning of second stage of development.
Functions: Female element in reproduction. Sensory and motor centre of "brain".
As in the higher animals, the female element of the termitary undergoes periodical
metamorphosis and has a far greater ontogenetic development than the male.

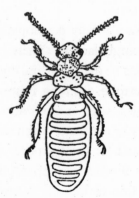

King (*Bellicosus* magnified.) Queen substitute. Similar to queen or king type,
except that the wings do not develop. *Function*: Sometimes used temporarily as
substitute for king or queen. Both sexes found.

satisfy the instinct, then she will discard the wings in one's hand. The observer must understand that it is absolutely necessary for her future life that she shall at least experience the impression of flight. If she has not this, she simply dies. Then she will never become a queen, her sexual life is ended. Sometimes even the struggle for freedom as her wings are held is sufficient to satisfy the instinct. Rapid and continuous movement of the wings while the insect remains stationary on a twig without actual flight through the air, also appears to satisfy occasionally. But these occurrences are more in the nature of exceptions. As a rule, there is complete frustration sexually if the insect has not flown and discarded her wings.

The king and queen look exactly alike and cannot be distinguished apart with the naked eye. They are the only perfectly formed insects in the termitary. They have fully developed eyes and although they were born and reared in darkness, they are highly pigmented. Black, brown and red colourings are found, which never appear in their children, except of course the future kings and queens.

The sexual organs are fully developed. Any natural means of defence is surprisingly lacking. There is probably no insect in our land which has so many natural enemies. One finds the true ant, not the termite, walking round boldly in the daylight, for only reptiles, such as frogs and lizards, which have no sense of taste, try to eat them. Their defence consists of an acid which is secreted for the purpose, and also an indigestible outer covering. So effective apparently are these methods of defence that we find certain beetles taking on the form of large ants so successfully that most animals are deceived by them. The unfortunate termite, on the other hand, is eaten greedily by all other animals. It is a remarkable lesson in nature study to watch the flight of the termites in uninhabited parts of Central Africa. Within a few minutes the surface of the earth is seething with living creatures coming to the feast. Out of the earth crawl frogs, toads, snakes, lizards and other reptiles. From where they receive the news I cannot tell. Even the tortoise appears. Other insects, crickets, beetles, centipedes, spiders, scorpions swarm in the grass. In the water, just below the surface, ones sees hundreds of fish and turtles. Out of the bushes slink jackals, cats, meercats, apes and monkeys. There is a temporary truce, except as regards the unfortunate flying termites. They appear to be going to fly merely to die. One begins to understand why nature produces them in such millions, notwithstanding the fact that each pair may be the origin of millions more. Every pair is necessary, because the slaughter is immense. One realizes now why the royal pair are in such a tremendous hurry after they have flown and discarded their wings. The only method of defence the flying termites make use of is flight after dusk. In this way they escape at least the birds which fly by day. But even this may not always happen. Sometimes the flight begins too early and in the twilight hundreds of hawks gather. The night hawks, owls and other night birds continue the feast into the darkest hours of the night.

One realizes that in this case there has been a displacement of the natural means of defence. What the individual king and queen have lost as regards natural means of defence is compensated for by the defences of the composite animal, the termitary. As soon as the community is formed, the termites never again appear in the daylight, except when injury necessitates this, and even then not in great numbers. However far they may have to go in search of food, and sometimes it may be hundreds of yards, they make underground passages in all directions, and the food itself is temporarily covered with cells and earth-work, making it unnecessary for any individual to appear in the open.

The same thing occurs with all other psychological charac-teristics and urges – they are shifted from the individual to the community. The individual termite is without feeling. For him there is no more pain. The injury of a group of termites, how-ever, is felt as pain by the community. The same thing occurs in the human body. The liver is incapable of feeling an injury. It is the human being, the composite animal, which becomes aware of the injury to the liver, as pain.

Neither does the individual termite feel hunger or thirst. If there is a famine, or if water begins getting scarce, the suffer-ing as such is felt only in the queen's chamber.

The mightiest urge of all, the sexual urge, does not exist in the individual. It has been set free from this irksome tie. The only vestige of self-government which appears to exist amongst the termites are the food, wound and danger signals which are sent out by the soldiers and answered by the work-ers. But this is no proof that the individual termite possesses a separate psyche. Apart from the power of locomotion, there is no vestige of this psyche. All actual motivations are direct-ed by signals from the queen's chamber.

These signals cease immediately the queen is destroyed and all directed activity ceases, even in the outlying sections of the termitary and even when these sections have been com-pletely isolated over a long period by a metal plate. This seems proof that the group movements, too, are directed by the queen, the brain of the termitary. The king and queen, deep in the absolute darkness of their chamber, bear in their persons two widely diverse functions, the mental and the sexual. The palace chamber is analogous to the skull in higher animals. Even the substance of the queen's body is reminiscent of the brain of mammals. All that is entirely lacking are the nerves which play such an important role in the physical economy of the more highly developed animals.

Having come to the conclusion that the termitary is a composite animal, the observer expects to find some trace at least of structures corresponding to nerves. A little consideration will enlighten one as to the reason why nothing of the kind is found. The most important function in man, for instance, of the nerves, is that of initiating and controlling movement and to carry impressions from the sense organs to the brain. On the other hand there are innumerable movements and functions in the human body which are directed and influenced by the brain without being actually linked up by nerves. I mentioned before this influence-at-a-distance which is found all over the body. The work and movements of the blood corpuscles, for instance, are set into being by an influence which is not material; so too are the special functions of the vital organs. The influence which streams from the queen is something intangible and similar to the influence-at-a-distance which directs so many functions in highly developed animals.

In a later chapter I will show how this mysterious influence has the power of penetrating all ordinary materials. For instance, it penetrates quite easily the thickest obtainable galvanized iron plates. Distance, however, lessens the power of the queen's influence. One may imagine Nature addressing the queen thus, after her short flight:

"Beloved, you are going to suffer a great loss. Instead of living in this glowing sunlight, you are going to spend your days in absolute darkness. Instead of the citizenship of the wide veld, instead of the freedom of the air, of mountains, trees and plains, you are going to spend your days as a prisoner in a narrow vault, in whose confines you will be unable to make the least movement. The annual return of the love season, the search for your beloved and the happy finding of your home and all the happiness bound up in this periodical stirring of the soul, of all this you are to be deprived. But in place of all this, you yourself will become a far more important and wonderful being. Although you will apparently be an immobile shapeless mass buried in a living grave, you will actually be a sensitive mainspring. You will become the feeling, the thinking, the seeing of a life a thousand times greater and more important than yours could ever have become. Above all, I will give you protection. The million dangers, the million enemies which threatened your life on every hand, will in your new life fling themselves in vain against your armour."

It was this need for protection which caused the development of the termitary. As individuals the queen and her subjects are the most threatened of all insects. As individuals, in an unprotected environment, the race would never have survived. As a composite animal, the termitary is very nearly perfectly protected. External wounds, destructive attacks which destroy the whole visible form of the termitary, do not touch its real life, which goes on as usual as though nothing untoward has happened. The wounds are merely repaired. The queen herself, as brain of the organism, is as well protected as the human brain in its skull. There are very few enemies which ever prove a real danger to the queen. One of the largest is the ant-eater; some of the most insidious are groups of beetles, which at times completely devastate a weakened termitary. This latter instance is analogous in every respect to the attack on the human body by pathological organisms. The termitary becomes diseased and dies.

Has the queen paid too dearly for protection? Nature answers this question in a different way from that in which we, or the queen, would.

"What matters it to me how much or how little is paid for the privilege of my protection? How much happiness is lost and how much misery the new life entails is of no importance What do I care for the individual? The race is safe, rejoicing, inexterminable. The individual must always pay, and no price is too high."

One realizes why development has taken this peculiar course, why at all costs the queen must remain immobile, why she has been imprisoned in a cell and has lost all power of locomotion. If she is the brain of the organism, that makes it all the more necessary for her to remain stationary in one place. The duplicate functions of the queen, mental and sexual, make matters more complicated. Movement appears to be an integral part of all sexual functions in nature. There seems to be a definite conflict here, but the development of the termitary has solved the problem. I shall not enlarge on this subject here. The student of nature will be aware of what happens, and even the uninitiated will find the solution if he compares this duplication of function in the termites with the same less developed complex in the bee queen. In the latter the sexual functions are the most important and the result is that the danger of the queen on her wedding flight becomes a danger to the whole hive. The termite queen is never again exposed to such danger, once the community is formed and she has been rendered immobile.

The human observer who watched the flight of the queen, who saw the glad meeting of the two sexes, who perhaps even lent a little human aid gives a sigh of relief when eventually the threatened pair find shelter in the protective lap of Mother Earth. Now at last they must be safe. Alas! Not yet. There is another great danger which threatens the birth of the new community. In our land it is a merciless enemy – we call it Drought. The termites must have water, more water, and still more water. As ninety per cent of their bodies consists of water the greatest part of their labour is concerned with the finding and carrying of water, on which the termitary is just as dependent as the warm-blooded animals are. The king and queen must find water immediately. They obtain this from damp earth. That is why the flight occurs only after heavy rains – this at least they expect from nature. Sometimes, however, they make a mistake. The first duty of the royal pair is to manufacture an organ for hatching out and feeding the first workers and soldiers. For this purpose a plentiful supply of water is necessary. If the water supply gives out during this initial period, all is finished; it means death to them and to the composite animal. Both king and queen work incessantly, making passages in the direction of moist earth. These generally descend perpendicularly and are the beginnings of the vertical aqueduct – at least in dry districts. At intervals in these first passages they make, or perhaps find, hollows in the earth and here they make their first termite gardens. Enthusiastic observers of the real ant have called them gardens, so we will continue using the term. They resemble very much our own agricultural efforts.

First the ground is carefully prepared. The fertilizer consists of finely chewed, partially digested vegetable substance, mostly dry wood and grass stalks. Then it is irrigated with water, much water, until the ground is saturated. Both king and queen labour incessantly; they do not rest for a second, nor do they sleep day or night. It is the last time, however, that they will ever be expected to work. The functions which they will fulfill in future can hardly be called work. At last the first garden is ready, deep in a hollow of one of the passages. No ray of light must ever fall upon it, everything is done in inky darkness. This first garden consists of a pat of cell structure and earth-work, and when it is well saturated, the two termites proceed to plant the seed of a peculiar fungus, which is to play an enormous role in the future life-history of the termitary and as such deserves our careful attention. I have said the termites plant the seed. I cannot, however, prove this to be a fact, but that is what appears to take place. They walk about on the damp garden and in the shortest possible time necessary for germination and development, the fungus springs up, in the form of a white mould. I have found the hyphae and spores of the fungus on the jaws and legs of flying termites immediately after they have left the termitary. It appears as though they purposely carry the seed to plant in the new

A close-up of a fungus garden.

A termitary split open to reveal the fungus gardens.

Termite damage in structural timber.

nest. One also finds spores on termites which have nothing to do with the gardens. In the neighbourhood of large termitaries one finds the spores in great numbers in the underground hollows and passages. They are spread by water, by wind, by worms and by insects. It is possible, therefore, that the spores might sow themselves on the specially prepared ground, without the assistance of the termite. The termites, however, do far more incredible things than the planting of these spores would be. So we will take it for granted that they do carry the spores and that the planting of the gardens is intentional.

Whether they do actually plant seed or not, there is certainly no question about the fertilization and irrigation of the gardens. The passage which leads to the water is constantly being deepened. While the damp earth is being excavated, the moisture is stored in the bodies of the two insects. The garden is irrigated with drops of a clear shining liquid, the same in all respects as that which is used for many other purposes later on by all the groups.

In this early garden, the queen lays her first eggs. At this stage she is still able to run about quickly and work actively. In the meantime wonderful things are happening to the fungus garden. The two insects do something to the mycelium of the plant which retards growth and development and at the same time the temperature of the garden begins to rise astoundingly.

The origin of this rise in temperature seems at first inexplicable. It cannot come from the termites, for their bodies are always at the same temperature as that of their environment. It comes from the garden, which functions as an incubator

101

and is responsible later for maintaining the heat of the composite animal. The normal temperature of the termitary taken in the queen's cell is from four to six degrees Fahrenheit higher than the normal temperature of a human being. There is little doubt that most of this heat is generated by the fungus-beds. It is well known that in all fungi rise of temperature takes place when the spores ripen. In the gardens of the termitary the temperature is kept raised to a certain degree by something the termite does to the plant which retards growth and development at the very stage when the fungi generate most heat. The garden, however, is more than incubator and nursery. The production of heat is a very important function, certainly, but in addition to this the garden becomes the stomach and liver of the composite animal.

By constant and rapid metabolism not only nutriment, but also digestive juices are assembled in the plant. Under the microscope and chemically one can find oil, protoplasm, glycogen, carbohydrates, proteid crystals, gum, alkaloids, and different enzymes, similar to those in the human body, which break up complicated sugars into dextrose and levulose, which reduce ordinary sugar to alcohol and carbon. The only substance we find no trace of is starch.

The circle or digestion takes place in this way: The workers and the king and queen in their first stages are the only termites in the nest which can masticate wood, grass-stalks and other coarse vegetable matter, and partially digest it. No other group in the termitary is able to absorb or digest anything but fluid. When the king and queen in their first stage, or the workers, have partially digested the food, it goes to the stomach and liver – the so-called gardens. Here it is further digested and changed by the fungi and the digestive juices I have mentioned. It happens in just the same way as in the human body. When the stomach and liver have prepared the food, it is taken up by the workers and soldiers in liquid form and becomes part of the whole circulation.

More than half this predigested food is used for building purposes. When one touches a newly built tower, one's fingers become sticky. With a magnifying glass one can see how each worker rolls the tiny grain in its jaws, coating it with the sticky fluid before placing it in position. This is the fluid which is obtained from the gardens. The water necessary for the production of this fluid is being constantly supplied to the gardens by a stream of workers, whose sole function appears to be this and the sowing of seed. If a vertical aqueduct is present, one finds a hollow every two or three feet, in which a small garden is cultivated. During severe droughts, water is constantly carried to the deepest gardens and the fungi there are kept alive. The great advantage of having little fungus beds so near to the water is obvious, as it spares the termites much labour. From these gardens the seed is carried to new ones, or to replant those which were killed by drought. These smaller gardens are never used for any other purpose; you will never find them used as nurseries, as is the case with the large gardens.

Another function of the fungus garden appears to be the isolation of colour. A dark-red colouring material can be obtained from them. It appears, therefore, that the termites find the red colouring matter of their bodies prepared for them by the gardens. The babies are entirely colourless, as one would expect from insects born in utter darkness. One would expect that they would never become coloured in the absence of light, and as they continue living in darkness it is difficult to explain the presence of all the brilliant tints. These, however, come from the gardens. The babies are white as milk until they are fed on the fungus fluid. Then only do we find their bodies assuming the blood-red colour of the adults.

10

PAIN AND TRAVAIL IN NATURE

We are now going to observe the conjugal behaviour of the king and queen in more detail, and will see three phenomena which are very wonderful. The word wonderful does not fit into science, for from one point of view every natural occurrence is as wonderful as another. But we are justified in using the term when we meet a phenomenon which is such an exception to the ordinary rules of nature that it appears to be a miracle. The early behaviour of the king and queen is a phenomenon of this kind. It reminds one of the fairy-godmother who waved her wand and turned the pumpkin into a coach and the mice into prancing steeds. The hidden meaning of what I am about to describe has escaped experienced observers. The naturalist Grassi studied these things in very favourable circumstances, but he did not fathom their meaning.

Much depends on the particular aspect in which the observer is interested. If one is interested in behaviourism, and has some knowledge of it, one sees much the entomologist overlooks. His powers of observation are trained to notice form; he is interested in naming and classifying; to him the dead insect is often of more worth than the living one. This does not mean that his work is of less importance; it may be of greater value than pure psychological investigation; and is far more difficult because less interesting. If, however, these things escape the experienced entomologist, it becomes necessary for us to take particular care lest we miss them too.

Up to the moment when the first garden has been made and planted and the first eggs are laid, the two insects, the king and queen, ordinary four-winged neuropterous insects, have been busy building their home, laying eggs like thousands of other insects around them. They have laid aside their wings, it is true, but they continue to behave like true winged insects. Then, however, strange things begin happening, so strange that we can hardly believe they actually occur.

While the queen is laying her eggs our searchlight disturbs her less than at any other time. It seems clear that her important work occupies her attention so deeply that even a cataclysm as the sudden flashing of an electric torch does not frighten her. She makes curious preparations. For a long while she stands on the place where the eggs are to be deposited, before she begins laying. Her body is in constant movement. The antennae sweep in circles and her jaws move ceaselessly. Occasionally she lifts the hinder part of her body in just the same way as she did when she was sending her first signal to her mate. Two or three times before the eggs actually are laid, she turns round and looks at the ground as if she expects to find something there. With the actual laying of the eggs the bodily contractions increase tremendously. When the first batch is laid, she turns round once more and examines them long and carefully. She touches them gently with her jaws and front legs, and then she lies motionless beside them for a time.

What does it all mean? We are here observing one of those wonders which I promised, and which is found in no other winged insect, nor in any other insect of similar development. Unless one has witnessed a similar occurrence in an animal a little higher in the scale of life, one cannot realize the significance of this behaviour. Actually we have witnessed the first appearance of a complex which plays a mighty role in the decadent and unnatural condition of the human race to-day. We are seeing the first evidence in nature of birth pangs. We think this cannot be the case in a winged insect. Surely it must be impossible. How can one tell that the queen's behaviour is due to pain?

One knows what usually happens in insects. The female builds a home, fills it with food, lays her eggs as easily and carelessly as if she were eating, drinking or cleaning her antennae. The male never appears on the scene. After the honeymoon his part of the work is done. The female's work also concludes with the building of the house and the laying of the eggs. She never sees her babies. She would not recognize them if she did, for how could she, a beautiful flying creature, have given birth to these odd little grubs, or wriggling worms?

Another thing. One has never seen a real insect baby. One expects it to be a caterpillar, then a cocoon, from which eventually comes the imago, the perfect insect, which does not differ from the parent. But a little white insect baby *is* found in the termite which does not undergo any further metamorphosis; which is born weak and helpless, and grows stronger slowly, just like a human baby. Does one see such anywhere else in the insect world?

There are instances of this, but never in an insect at the same stage of development as the termite queen. Let us turn to the study of the behaviour of another creature, which is zoologically classified near the insects, but which psychologically should be in the mammal class. I am referring to the South African scorpion.

Among my tame scorpions there was a gigantic female which gained a good deal of fame. She was five and a half inches long. She first introduced herself to Mr. Charlie Pienaar, by killing a full-fledged chicken in his presence. She tackled the chicken's leg, clung on, and gave one sting of her deadly lance, just above the joint. Within a few seconds the chicken was paralysed and was dead in ten minutes. Later on she became so tame and knew me so well that I could push a finger before her suddenly and allow her to grip me with her claws. She would bring her sting into contact with my skin, before recognizing me. Immediately she would relax and withdraw her dangerous weapon. I could handle her freely. She liked being scratched gently. Shortly after she came into my possession I noticed that an interesting event was shortly to take place. I watched her continually and gave her every care, for I wished to observe every stage of the process. I must admit that in those days I knew so little zoology that I expected to see her lay eggs. I was astounded therefore to see her give birth to sixteen living babies. Fully harnessed and spurred they made their entry by pairs, small white helpless babies – but perfect little scorpions. There was no doubt at all that the delivery caused the mother much pain. I remember a woman asking me anxiously whether the young ones were born with pincers and stings, and then

108

giving a prayer of thanks that human babies at least do not possess these.

What seemed very strange, too, was that the scorpion mother loved her queer little youngsters. Very carefully she helped them on to her back, where they remained sitting in two rows with their heads and pincers directed outwards and their tails interlaced behind them. I knew her well enough to tell by her behaviour that she would not allow any handling of her babies, so I did not risk doing this until they were fully grown. The mother would tear their food into small pieces and feed them carefully, while above them she waved her sting defensively. A more loving mother you will find nowhere else in nature.

It immediately seemed that one was dealing here with one of nature's deepest mysteries, and that we were nearing the boundaries of yet unexplored country. Of the appearance of pain in nature, no satisfactory explanation has yet been given. Many theories have been formulated, some of them probably bordering on the truth, but I know of no naturalist who has given a well-grounded and true analysis of the subject. Those who have, by original research, even approached the secret of birth pain, can be counted on the fingers of one hand.

One realizes that birth pain is a great mystery. One knows that pain in general is a warning signal to living creatures. If pain were to disappear from this earth, life would soon cease. Without pain organic matter cannot exist. Everywhere in nature pain acts as a defence – except in the case of birth. Why then do we find this agony of suffering at the birth of highly developed animals? It plays such an important part and is so common that it must have some equally important

purpose. What purpose had natural selection when she allowed this amazing exception to the general rule? Birth pain is
clearly not protective; indeed, it is the very opposite. One can
often learn the meaning of normal phenomena best by observing what happens in unnatural and abnormal manifesta-
tions of the same thing. One knows that in apes, in tame animals and in humans, the mechanism which causes birth pains
may be a danger to the lives of both mother and child. Yet
birth is the great end of the struggle for existence, the event
which nature, as it were, considers the first and most important, which would protect with all her powers and would make
safe for mother and child. Why should it be coupled with vio-
lent and non-protective suffering, which increases as you
mount the scale of life? What does this mean? We will follow
the path of pain as it winds the way through the dark ages.

With an ordinary immersion lens dipped in a drop of stagnant water from a cattle kraal, for one *can* see life with an
immersion lens without stain or oil, I watched the movements
of *Volvox* and *Amoeba* for hours on end. Many unnatural conditions in their environment may be brought about. A red-hot
needle pressed against the glass will cause a sudden rise in
temperature of water film, enough to cause the death of a unicellular organism. One can introduce strychnine, carbolic
acid, or arsenic over the outer edge of the film. A strong ray
of red light, sharper than a needle point played over the film
will also kill the organisms. In these experiments one gains a
certain insight. One sees the unicellular animals start and
retract from the dangers you have caused. If you study similar instances in higher animals, you find that nature guards
the way to death by pain.

On the unaffected side of your film you see the cells budding, dividing and multiplying.

Someone once said that all behaviourism in nature could be referred to hunger. This saying has been repeated thousands of times yet is false. Hunger itself is pain – the most severe pain in its later stages that the body knows except thirst, which is even worse. Love may be regarded as a hunger, but it is not pain.

What protects animals, what enables them to continue living, what assures the propagation of the race? A certain attribute of organic matter. As soon as one finds life, one finds this attribute. It is inherent in life; like most natural phenomena it is polarized, there is a negative and a positive pole. The negative pole is pain, the positive pole is sex. This attribute may be called the saving attribute of life; and it is here where one comes closest to what appears like a common purpose beyond nature.

All animals, large and small, possess some mechanism for feeling pain, and this pain always acts as a safeguard against death. An animal struggles to get out of the water, not because he is afraid of death – of which he knows nothing – but because the first stages of drowning are extremely painful. Close to the pole of pain we find fear as another urge towards certain behaviour. The other pole, sex, is more complicated – the final result of it is mother love.

In the apes, in a lesser degree, and in man, in the highest degree, there has been a great degeneration of both poles. In man there exists no longer any selective power against the attack of pathological organisms and thousands of organic diseases. The result is that the mechanism of pain, which

111

developed only as a defence in nature, is brought into action uselessly as a result of the ills man is heir to, and from which animals in natural environments are free. Sex has become degenerate in man to the same degree. In nature, the sexual urge, like other race memories, needs an external stimulus before it is roused. As we have seen, this is scent alone in most mammals. Sometimes scent and colour go paired. In such cases we find brilliant colourings in the female as well as scent. In such animals destruction of the olfactory sense in the male means the end of sex.

In the ape and man we find the first animals, excluding tame animals, in which sex can be roused without an external stimulus. The reason for this is one that has been mentioned before. In man and the apes all perceptions, all experiences are registered as individual causal memories. The cortex of the brain is the organ of this function. The first awareness of sex must be transmitted through the cortex as an ordinary causal environmental memory where it is immediately absorbed as a separate memory. The ape and man remember this as a pleasurable experience to which they can react at will. The result is that the greatest of all natural laws, periodicity, is lost in the human race. The periodic organic condition, which should rouse the sexual sense, has become an absolutely useless, degenerate, pathological manifestation. The ultimate result, birth, which in all other animals is safe and certain, has become in the human a major surgical operation, where the lives of both mother and child are endangered. Without skilled help in labour the civilized races would vanish from the earth in three generations, said a famous German obstetrician. Two-thirds of all the organic and mental disease of man may be ascribed to the degeneracy of the sexual sense, said another expert.

A little way behind man we find apes, with similar degeneracy and similar results, only in a lesser grade. We have taken a brief and general glance at the two poles, pain and sex. There still remains the mysterious exception, birth pain. We realize at once that this has no connection with protective pain. It guards no road leading to death; no animal can escape from it. We have learnt the general rule that every instinctive action is unlocked by one and only one key. We have seen how in the termite the stimulus or key to sex is flight, and in the kudu scent; how the whole aquatic life of the otter is initiated by the sight and touch of water. In exactly the same way we find that birth pain is the key which unlocks the doors to mother love, in all animals from the termite queen to the whale. Where pain is negligible, mother love and care are feeble. Where pain is absent, there is absolutely no mother love. During a period of ten years' observation, I found no single exception to this rule. Some naturalist once suggested that the function of birth pain was to draw the attention of the mother to the young one. This is not so. There is no such thing as "drawing attention" in the instinctive soul. The unlocking of the mother love complex through pain is beyond consciousness, beyond the knowledge of the mother and has nothing to do with drawing her attention to her offspring. Naturally it was not enough to show the connection between birth pain and mother love in order to prove that one was the result of the other. A large number of experiments dispelled all doubt. The following notes will explain the general principle.

113

For the experiment I used a herd of sixty half-wild buck, known in South Africa as Kaffir Buck. I have proof that during the previous fifteen years there had been no single instance of a mother refusing her young in normal circumstances.

1. Six cases of birth during full anaesthesia of the mother induced by chloroform and ether; unconsciousness in no case lasted for more than twenty-five minutes after delivery. In all six cases the mother refused to accept the lamb of her own volition.
2. Four cases of birth during paralysis – consciousness and feeling were partly paralysed but not destroyed by the American arrow poison curare. In all four cases the mother appeared for over an hour in great doubt as to the acceptance of her lamb. After this period, three mothers accepted their lambs; one refused it.

    To prove that refusal on the part of these mothers was not due to the general disturbance caused by the anaesthetics used, I did the following experiments:
3. In six cases of birth the mother was put under chloroform anaesthesia immediately after delivery was complete but before she had seen her lamb. Unconsciousness lasted about half an hour. In all six cases the mother accepted her lamb without any doubt immediately after she became conscious. Similar experiments with curare gave the same result.

From these and other experiments I became convinced that without pain there can be no mother love in nature, and this pain must actually be experienced psychologically. It is not sufficient for the body to experience it physiologically.

Mother love is a psychological complex, therefore the key which makes it function must be a psychological one, analogous to the psychological impression of flight in the case of the termite.

We have seen what the result of birth pain was in the case of the scorpion mother. In a later chapter we will see the interesting way in which the same principle is verified in the termite queen.

This complex, as we find in all such complexes of the instinctive soul, has long ago ceased functioning in the human. Birth pain has become psychologically a useless rudimentary manifestation, which now is a source of danger, like most rudimentary organs.

One expert has written: "When nature wishes to annihilate a race, the first attack made is in the direction of the sexual sense." This is said in topsy-turvy fashion, and I am not sure whether it is true. But one fact is clear, the degeneration of the sexual sense is responsible for the greatest part of human suffering. Yet one part of sex, mother love, gave a twist to man's psychological development which was largely responsible for his domination of the earth.

11

Uninherited Instincts

I have said that in the termite queen, pain accompanied the laying of the first eggs. It is usually very difficult to be certain of the perception of pain in the animal world, for the outward signs vary enormously in different races and in varying circumstances. In general, however, one may say that the outward signs of pain are more or less similar in all higher animals. If an animal is wrung by convulsive spasms, makes needless movements of its limbs, draws back the head, and at the same time moans and groans, one recognizes that it is in pain, although one may not know the cause of the pain. This expression of pain is an international language amongst animals, and even man knows it from childhood. Most insects speak the same language, without, however, the audible sounds. Therefore anyone, watching the bodily movements of the queen termite which I have described, will feel certain they are the expression of pain. If one is in any doubt, one can dispel this by actually hurting the queen and comparing her behaviour with that which occurs when she is laying her first eggs. Touch certain parts of her body with a glass rod dipped in sulphuric acid and immediately we see the identical waving of the antennae, the writhing of the body, and so on, exactly what happens when she is laying her eggs.

The greatest proof to me, however, was found in her behaviour after her eggs were laid. It is not scientific proof of course. I am trying to establish the connection between the cause and the effect, and now I am taking the effect as proof of the cause. Yet everyone will grant that a general knowledge of animal behaviour can find proof in itself. When I say that as soon as I observed the bodily movements of the queen, I immediately realized that she was in pain, and that I then could prophesy that as a result of this she would in all probability show signs of affection for her young. Although both occurrences were so improbable, it only indicated that I possessed some special fragment of knowledge which could, if necessary, produce proof. Long before I made acquaintance with the queen in travail, I had come to the conclusion that birth pain was the key to mother love. Let us watch her behaviour immediately afterwards.

On the little garden patch where the first eggs are laid, we see the king and queen continually wandering around. They are busy irrigating and fertilizing the fungi-beds. Soon the first larvae appear. We see them wriggling in the garden, small, white, helpless babies, but we can already distinguish the different kinds, the so-called soldiers and the mandibulated workers. The queen appears among them. We see something glisten in her jaws. In the stream of light it looks transparent and pure as a diamond. Under the magnifying glass we see it is a drop of fluid. She approaches one baby after another, they lift their heads and you see the drop disappear. The queen is busy feeding her little ones.

As I said before, behaviour such as this is unknown in insects at the same stage of development. The nearest approach to similarity is the statement of von Buttel-Reepen that a certain bee, *Halictus,* lays her eggs so slowly that the first eggs hatch before she has laid the last, and that she therefore comes in touch with her own living young. I think that in that case it is sheer chance; but even that instance is so exceptional that stress must be laid on it. Of care and feeding, however, there is no mention.

With this feeding and preparation of the first soldiers and workers, the individual labour of the king and queen comes to an end, and so does our own opportunity for observation. From now on the community suffers from photophobia – fear of light – to such an extent that the usual methods of observation are impossible. This draws our attention to a phenomenon which is as mysterious as the transference of the queen from cell to cell. The king and queen do not possess this instinctive photophobia. They are ordinary winged insects, and only a short while before we saw them in the sunlight flying around. The soldiers and workers, on the contrary, are totally blind and hate the light. How can they possibly inherit a hereditary instinct which the parents do not possess? Nor is this all. The soldiers and workers inherit many instincts which the parents do not possess. They begin immediately building complicated structures. They make cells, passages, aqueducts and a crust containing various forms of arch. One can separate a part of the termitary with a steel plate, in such a fashion that there is no communication between the termites on each side of it. Nevertheless the same curve of arch, or a lower one, as the case may be, is built on either side of

118

the plate. They become aware of the presence or absence of light on the surface through twelve inches of opaque earth. They manufacture cardboard from grass-stalks and wood. They steal eggs from other termites and carry them to the breeding chambers and care for them. They take care of the larvae and feed them, but this is of course an instinct which the queen possesses. They make gardens and replant dried-up gardens. From whom do they inherit these hereditary instincts? All soldiers and workers have the same instincts. Throughout nature we find hereditary instincts of this kind inherited by an organism only from parents with similar instincts. Whence come the special instincts of the sexless forms in the community? The king and queen cannot hand them on, because they themselves do not possess them, nor do they take part in or come in touch with the communal life of their citizens; the soldiers and workers cannot hand on their instincts to other soldiers and workers, for they take no part in the reproduction of the race.

I must admit that all this has never seemed a mystery to me, for I felt I had long ago discovered the secret. When one knows the answer to a problem, it can never appear impossible to solve.

In some ways this is the most mysterious occurrence in the life-history of the termite. It deserves careful attention. It is a strange and interesting fact that inexperienced observers seldom become aware of these mysteries, still less do they seek an explanation.

In connection with this riddle, I want to show how modern European learning handles cases of this kind, and the explanation it finds. I am able to do this through the kindness

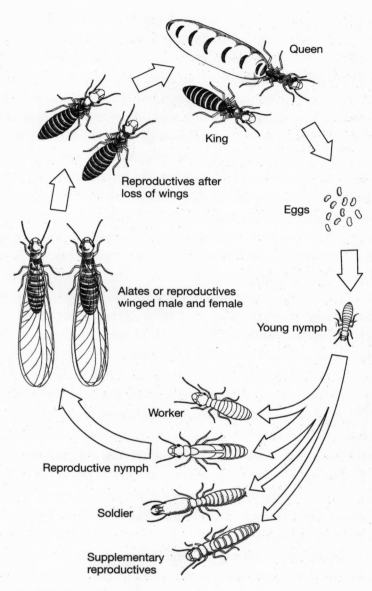

Queen

King

Reproductives after
loss of wings

Eggs

Alates or reproductives
winged male and female

Young nymph

Worker

Reproductive nymph

Soldier

Supplementary
reproductives

The life cycle of termites.

120

of a correspondent, personally unknown to me, who sent me a monograph written by Professor Dr. Bugnion of the University of Lausanne. Dr. Bugnion has studied termites in Ceylon for some years, and this monograph is to form part of a monumental work of the famous psychologist Auguste Forel. The title is *The Community World of the Termite*. Dr. Bugnion discusses in particular the wars between the ants and the termites, with special reference to the origin of instinct. As would be the case in any tropical country, Dr. Bugnion saw many instances of attacks on termites by ants. He ascribes all the instincts and the variations in form of the termites to this continuous state of warfare. I must state at once that I had practically no evidence of this ant warfare in Waterberg. On the contrary, we know that one of the nimblest and most ferocious of our flesh-eating ants lives by choice in a termitary belonging to one of the most helpless of termites which possesses no soldier class. If we break open such a termitary, it is easy to get an impression of war, which nevertheless is based on inaccurate observation. There is no war; in fact most probably it is protection and friendship. This may be proved by anyone who cares to do so. If we break down a number of the smaller termitaries, sooner or later we come upon one which ants and termites occupy together. Of this small, pale termite there is only one class, the worker. Look at them under a magnifying glass. Their manner of building is entirely different from that of the termite we have studied hitherto. The workers appear immediately at the edge of the wound. But they do not carry stones and stick these together to mend the breach. These pale termites build with clay only. Each worker who appears at the margin of the wound tests a place with his jaws, swings round with a characteristic movement and deposits a small layer of clean soft mud. Sometimes he deposits just a spot, more frequently a little layer. Dr. Bugnion had the opportunity of seeing the collection of this mud, but he could not actually see what the termites were doing. What I have told will enable everyone to recognize this particular termite. Among the termitaries broken into, we are sure to find one where a section is inhabited by a dark grey ant, nimble, ferocious and excited. At first sight it appears very much as though these ants are bent on slaughter. They run rapidly between and over the termites, apparently inspired with terror and fury. Occasionally one of them will seize a termite and carry him a short distance. Sometimes a termite will grip the leg of an ant and be dragged about without apparently causing the ant any inconvenience. The wounded termites also are seized and dragged about. In the meantime the other termites quite peacefully go about their business of repairing their fortifications. The ants continually touch and test the repairs, but they never attempt to throng into the passages or to hinder the workers in any way. They appear to have special entrances to the innermost parts of the nest. The observer speedily comes to the conclusion that there is here nothing comparable to murder or war. What it actually was I had no opportunity of discovering. Much time is necessary to study even a single phenomenon of termite behaviour in a dry country like South Africa. I believe this communal life of termite and ant, whatever its basis may be, holds many surprises in store for scientists. We find, however, in South Africa little evidence of the tropical strife of which Dr. Bugnion speaks, and realize that it is extremely easy to come to unsound conclusions.

In a later chapter I will try to interpret these first labours of the king and queen. At present it is sufficient to say that with the attainment of adult stature by the workers and soldiers, systematic observation becomes impossible. The first and most important reason for this is the photophobia already mentioned. All the first efforts of the workers and soldiers are concentrated on sealing up all holes by which light can enter or the observer can watch them. If one perseveres and reopens these holes, the termites simply vanish and that is the end of the nest which took so much time and patience to bring into being. It is possible, however, by breaking into many termitaries to form a fairly accurate picture in our minds of the further course of events in the community. A cement chamber is made for the queen and she is imprisoned there. Passages are made in all directions for the conveyance of coarse food to the different digestive centres; gardens are cultivated on a large scale and planted with fungi; construction of the superficial defensive crust forms an important part of their work.

To come back to this great mystery of inherited instinct. Every organism, excepting the apes and man, inherits from its parents all the instincts, that is hereditary environmental memory, which it needs for its own struggle for existence. It is born with the knowledge of what kind of food it needs, where and how to obtain it; it knows its natural enemies and how to defend itself against them; it knows how to make a nest or other home; how to feed its little ones and to care for them. All this knowledge is there without the

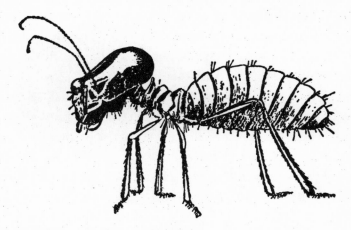

(*Eutermes* or *Trinervitermes*.) Mandibulated worker; water carrier, mason, probably also gardener, nurse and feeder. One of its most important functions is to bring all coarse foodstuff into the general metabolism. These workers form part of what corresponds to the blood-stream in higher animals. *Colour*: Somewhat etiolated with light-red markings. Blind, no organs of hearing, sexless.

organism having to learn it, without even coming into touch with the other individuals of its race. I gave an interesting example of this in the South African yellow weaver bird, which, after being kept out of its natural environment for four generations, by hatching the eggs under canaries, instinctively knew how to build its characteristic nest and how to feed its young.

No one taught these birds. Four generations of their ancestors had never seen a plaited nest or tasted a worm, yet the fifth generation remembered what to do. This is what is called instinct or hereditary environmental memory. In the termite we find three apparently different insects – the queens, the workers and the soldiers, being produced from one father and

124

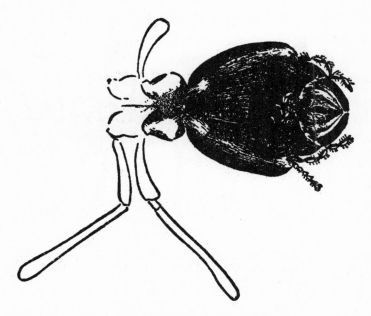

Head of *Eutermes* worker from below, showing the mouth parts.
These are specially developed for purposes of building and feeding.

mother who are completely different from two of their offspring. If one did not actually know the contrary one would
believe the inmates of the termitary to be completely different
insects.

With the physical differences go special hereditary memories or instincts. The soldier is armed with the first hypoder-
mic syringe made by nature, which she eventually perfected
in the poison fangs of the adder. In his polished head the termite soldier carries a little flask of poison and on his forehead
a needle-like tube through which the sticky fluid is squirted.
He uses his weapon only against threatening enemies or
strangers. The worker has strong, well-made jaws and a glue-

125

producing gland which he uses to construct most complicated building operations. As soon as he has reached adult stature he begins to make gardens, care for and feed the king and queen, tend the hatching eggs, carry food and partially digest it for the benefit of the whole republic. Both these insects are totally blind, neither of them possesses eyes or other organs of sense; nevertheless they are aware of the presence or absence of light through twenty-four inches of compact earth.

12

THE MYSTERIOUS POWER
WHICH GOVERNS

The termites dig deep boreholes to find water, and from this source it is conveyed for general purposes. When a breach is made in a termitary, the syringe-bearing or nasicorn soldiers are the first to appear. They inspect the damage slowly and thoughtfully from all sides. If there are no workers at hand, or only a few, the soldiers begin to signal. By quick movements of the throat plates of their armour, they make a sound, a sudden *tik-tik-tik*. In houses infested by termites, this sound can be heard at night in all directions. By this signal the soldiers summon the workers to the place of attack. The same sound is used as food signal. So urgent is this call that even workers who have been appointed to special tasks, like conveying water, carrying the larvae, gardening, feeding of the royal pair, drop their work and throng to the place from where the alarm has sounded. As I have shown before, the behaviour of the two kinds of termite corresponds in every respect to the functions of the blood corpuscles in higher animals. Just as the white corpuscles make a cordon round the wound, which the red corpuscles begin healing, so the soldiers form a protective circle while the workers repair the breach. If you annoy the soldiers individually with a sharp

Eutermes nasicorn soldier, with syringe. Blind, deaf, sexless. Colour: Head, reddish-yellow; body, blood red. Generally highly pigmented. Mouth parts, rudimentary. *Function*: 1. Part of the "blood-stream". 2. Defence, when outer layer of termitary is attacked.

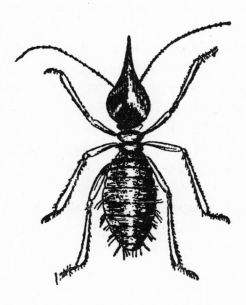

Eutermes nasicorn soldier seen from above.

128

object like a needle, they go into a kind of convulsion. Their bodies are jerked angrily from side to side and through the syringe-like weapon they squirt a drop of clear sticky fluid in the direction of the danger. This fluid appears to cause extreme pain to other small insects, glues together their jaws and legs and renders them helpless. All these actions are instinctive.

Now we return to the question: Where do they get these instincts? That their behaviour must be inherited cannot be doubted, because all the workers and soldiers possess exactly the same instincts as the others of their type. It is impossible for them to have inherited these from their father and mother, because neither the king nor the queen possesses any of these instincts. The royal pair possess perfect eyes and do not fear the light as the workers and soldiers do. On the other hand they do not possess a special, but inexplicable sense which enables them to perceive the dimmest ray of light as their children do. They know nothing of collective building of termitaries, of squirting poison, or carrying water. They do not even come in touch with the labours of the community; we appear to be forced to the conclusion that the workers and soldiers inherit a large number of environmental memories which none of their ancestors ever possessed. On the other hand they do not inherit one of the special instincts of their father and mother, for they cannot fly, never copulate and never lay eggs. They themselves cannot hand on their instincts to other soldiers and workers, for they never produce young. It appears to be a paradox!

Let us see what were the observations of Dr. Bugnion of Ceylon, and how he explained the mystery. I will quote what

129

Head of *Eutermes* soldier from below, showing rudimentary mouth parts.
In the ampulla is stored the glutinous liquid used in defence.

he says about his difficulties, and discuss his theories, and then give my own criticism of them.

He says:

"When the biologist, having satisfied himself that (1) the soldiers who are trusted with the task of defence, are totally blind, and that (2) the workers who do the repairs are small, insignificant insects, not more than five millimetres in length, when he sees the collective drive of the termites, he becomes perplexed and amazed. His wonder increases when he tries to discover the power that governs the termites and the moral law which binds them together – and finds no trace of it."

It is difficult to understand exactly what Dr. Bugnion means. I think what he meant to say was: "The biologist clearly sees the effects of a governing power and a moral bond."

130

What the biologist does not discover so easily is the source of this governing power and moral bond.

Dr. Bugnion continues:

"Finally, the biologist is forced to conclude that the activity of these little insects, which appear to behave so intelligently and thoughtfully, is entirely instinctive."

I must admit that intelligence and thoughtfulness, as we humans understand these, never entered my mind in connection with the termites. Perhaps I was lucky enough to discover the secret of the behaviour of the termites too soon for that; and perhaps I knew just sufficient about behaviourism in animals to prevent me from going too far astray. I say this in all humility. I know it is extremely easy to go astray in what we call comparative psychology, when one has had little opportunity of learning to know animals in their natural surroundings and when one uses human intelligence as the criterion of judgment.

In describing the wonderful collective activity of the workers and soldiers, Dr. Bugnion says:

"It is amazing how they can do all this without a single mistake." He is wrong, however, for they make many mistakes. They often go to work mistakenly and persevere in their mistakes. Remember the useless turrets in this respect, excrescences forming a danger to the community. As clever as they are in one direction, just so unbelievably stupid are they in other directions. On the other hand, Dr. Bugnion must have missed perceiving the real building genius which the termite possesses, or else he would not have risked giving so decided and confident an explanation as he gives us later. The solution given above, of course, is not very convincing. To say that the

131

work of the termites is instinctive is like trying to explain the nature of wind by saying it is *wind*. The actual problem confronting us is not whether the activity of the termites is governed by the reason or instinct, but who is the architect who designs the plans which the workers execute. Let us look at the workers through a magnifying glass. We see them appear one by one from the dark depths, each carrying a tiny grain of earth. Without the least thought, each worker rolls the pebble round and round in its jaws. It covers it with a sticky mucilage, sets it in position in the breach and vanishes again into the depths. No reasonable person can imagine for one moment that every small worker is conscious of the purpose of its work, that it carries in its mind the plan, or even part of the plan of the building operations. The tower or breach may be a million times larger than the termite itself. The workers attack the repairs from every side, and are totally blind. We can convince ourselves that the termites at one side of the breach never come into contact with those on the other side. They may fetch their materials from different parts of the nest. If we have any doubt of this we can easily dispel it. Take a steel plate a few feet wider and higher than the termitary. Drive it right through the centre of the breach you have made, in such a way that you divide both the wound and the termitary into two separate parts. One section of the community can never be in touch with the other, and one of the sections will be separated from the queen's cell. The builders on one side of the breach know nothing of those on the other side. In spite of this the termites build a similar arch or tower on each side of the plate. When eventually you withdraw the plate, the two halves match perfectly after the dividing cut has been repaired. We cannot escape the ultimate conclusion that somewhere there exists a preconceived plan which the termites merely execute. Where is the soul, the psyche, in which this preconception exists? That is the problem which must be solved. Dr. Bugnion says it is instinct. If we accept that, then *whose* instinct? Does he maintain that every tiny worker carries part of the plan in its little soul? The experiment with the steel plate disposes of this theory. Even if one could prove that every worker had an instinctive knowledge of part of the plan, then the ultimate problem would still remain unsolved.

Where does each worker obtain his part of the general design? We can drive in the steel plate and then make a breach on either side and still the termites build identical structures on each side. It cannot be an inherited tendency, for the termites do not always build the same kind of arch or other structure. We can find a dozen different widths of arch near the surface of a large termitary. These arches are one of the amazing features of the termites' building powers. It cannot be due to the instinctive knowledge of the individual termite. If the termite always built one kind of form, one kind of tower, one kind of arch, we might perhaps come to the conclusion that it worked according to instinctive or inherited knowledge. Even then a doubt would exist. We are inclined to imagine the termites thinking and reasoning in our own way. Yet we know that they possess perceptive powers a million times more acute than our own senses. They become aware, for instance, by a fleeting touch of another termite, that he belongs to their own nest. They then follow his trail towards food, with unfailing certainty. From this has arisen the theory of "intelligent communication" which Dr. Bugnion and even

Forel still appear to credit. By touch, they can perceive alarm and agitation in a comrade and can apparently tell where the danger lies. They become aware over incredible distances of the signals of the soldiers; all these things they sense without a vestige of a sense organ.

How can one compare this soul with that of a human being? When one sees a tiny worker hastily placing a single grain of sand on the wall of a building which eventually will become a massive tower twelve or fifteen feet high, millions upon millions of times larger than itself, can one assume for one moment that the worker knows, in the human sense, what the final result of its work is going to be? If this were so its intelligence would be that of a god, compared with our own. His work is naturally due to instinct, as Dr. Bugnion says, but it is not the instinct of the worker. It is the instinct and design of a separate soul situated outside the individual termite.

If we carry our recent experiment a little further, new light begins to trickle through on our problem.

While the termites are carrying on their work of restoration on either side of the steel plate, dig a furrow enabling you to reach the queen's cell, disturbing the nest as little as possible. Expose the queen and destroy her. Immediately the whole community ceases work on either side of the plate. We can separate the termites from the queen for months by means of this plate, yet in spite of that they continue working systematically while she is alive in her cell; destroy or remove her, however, and their activity is at an end.

If the termitary under observation is in the neighbourhood of other termitaries, we can establish a few more facts experimentally. If there is a termitary within a yard or two one can prove that the termites of both nests mix freely without fighting. Place a piece of wood equidistant from both nests and spray the ground around it with water. If you expose the passages you will find that termites from both nests are destroying the wood. If you break into these two termitaries and put workers and soldiers from one nest into the other, you will find they do not get attacked. If, however, you do the same to termitaries twenty or thirty yards from each other, then the strangers are pounced on immediately by workers and soldiers and killed. If you destroy the queen in one of the two nests adjoining each other, then the termites of that nest cease work and move to the adjoining nest where they apparently swear allegiance to the new queen. If, however, you destroy the queen of a nest which is some distance from another, the termites make no attempt to transfer to another nest, but die in their old home. The reason for this difference in conduct is, I think, this: The mysterious power which streams from the queen functions only within a limited distance. Every termite is under the influence of this power. If their two termitaries are situated close to each other, the power of each queen operates in both nests. It is through this psychological power of the queen that the termites of one nest are capable of recognizing their fellow-citizens and discovering strange intruders.

The following control experiment shows this clearly.

Take soldiers and workers from one nest and place them in a far distant nest and make certain that they really are attacked, by waiting until the disturbance caused by the breach has died down; then destroy the queen of the first nest. If you transfer termites as before immediately after you have

135

killed the queen, you will find they are again attacked. If, however, you wait a day or two and then transfer the termites, they are no longer attacked, but are accepted as new citizens of the republic.

It appears therefore as if the workers and soldiers carry with them *something* of their own queen. We will assume it is something analogous to scent. Personally I do not think it is scent but something much more subtle. But if we think of it as scent it will simplify matters, for we are actually dealing with something far and away beyond human senses.

The power of the queen reaches only certain fixed limits. It can penetrate earth, rock and even metal plates. It evaporates within one or two days. It is the mainspring of all the collective activity of the soldiers and workers. The queen is the psychological centre of the community; she is the brain of the organism which we call a termitary.

From this shapeless, immobile object, imprisoned in her narrow vault, there emanates a power which directs all the activities of her subjects, just as our own brain rules the functions of the blood corpuscles and regulates and keeps in order the composite animal we call our body.

Dr. Bugnion never discovered the psychological functions of the queen. He assumed that the king and queen possess only sexual functions. He therefore is checked by all kinds of inexplicable difficulties which simply do not exist for me, and the explanations which he gives are at times ludicrous. If only he had had the opportunity of accompanying a professional South African termite-catcher he would without any doubt have discovered the secret. This chance I was fortunate enough to have had. His greatest difficulty was the problem of where the soldiers and workers get their hereditary memory. He found two solutions. The first was founded on the fact that some observers discovered individuals of the sexless forms possessing perfect organs. He assumed, therefore, that the sexless forms were at one time fertile. Then he says:

"Given these facts, we have only to conceive of the period during which the defence methods were perfected as coinciding with the period during which the workers and soldiers were fertile in order to render more plausible the hereditary transmission of the improvements in question and of the instincts (neoform) related to them."

If this is so, he must accept the theory that the present queen and king types are descended from the present sexless types. That cannot be true, instead the very opposite is actually the case. I do not think anyone can fail to accept the theory that the termite was originally a single flying insect of the same type as the present king and queen. The founding of community life was the cause of the physical differentiation into workers and soldiers. With these changes new instincts arose. The laying of eggs by workers is a very rare occurrence. One also occasionally finds rudimentary eyes and wing-buds in a few soldiers. These are all atavisms, which show that the original termite was a fertile flying insect. One thing is certain, both the changed physical characteristics and the new instincts are transmitted by the queen, although she does not possess, nor did she ever possess, either of these things herself.

There is another fact which Dr. Bugnion has not touched on. How does it happen that the soldiers and workers not only inherit instincts which their father and mother did *not* possess, but also do *not* inherit the specialized instincts the father and mother *do* possess?

The second explanation which Dr. Bugnion puts forward is somewhat surprising. He must have been very much mystified when he wrote the following:

"As the workers and soldiers live in the interior of the compartments in the company of the sexual forms until the moment of swarming, it is not entirely incredible, judging by the above suggestion [that the ants and termites carry on intelligent communication with each other], that while they are living together they should exchange a few ideas. As a result of these communications new instincts acquired by the workers and soldiers would become the property of the community as a whole."

If Dr. Bugnion had said that he had seen a termite soldier giving birth to a whale it would not have sounded more "entirely incredible" than the above statement. The workers and soldiers are supposed to tell their work and plans to the queen. She remembers what she is told and conveys this garnered knowledge to later workers and soldiers born to her. Dr. Bugnion still believes in the "intelligent communication" of ants and termites. He calls it "antennae-language". I was under the impression that this fairy tale had been relegated to the nursery where it belongs. Everyone should be convinced by now, I hope, that there is only one conclusion which accords with all our knowledge of termite behaviour: The individual worker or soldier possesses no individual instincts. He forms part of a separate organism of which the queen is the psychological centre. The queen has the power, call it instinct if you will, of influencing the soldiers and workers in a certain way, which enables them to perform collective duties. This power or instinct she transmits to all queens born from her. As soon as the queen is destroyed all the instincts of workers and soldiers cease immediately. She transmits this psychological power to the future queens just as she transmits to them the power of producing three infinitely differing forms of insect: the queen, the worker and the soldier.

At times Dr. Bugnion comes extraordinarily near to discovering the secret. He says:

"The multifarious duties, which are carried out under our eyes by the soldiers on the one hand and the workers on the other, give us the illusion of a higher direction, whereas in reality this direction does not exist, or if it does exist resides solely in the community as a whole."

Again later he says:

"The male and female individuals which are described in the higher termites as king and queen, have no authority and possess no power of any kind. The king and queen termite shut in their closed cell do not even know what is happening outside. It would be impossible for them to give orders from the depths of their prison."

One notices that Dr. Bugnion constantly talks of the termites as if they have human understanding: "to know and to give orders"! He thinks anthropomorphically all the time. He assumes that the termites are able to "talk", but that touch is necessary for this. He does not think of a subtle immaterial influence which functions at a distance. If only he had put this question to himself: How does the queen hold the community together from her cell in the depths? There are millions of her subjects which never come in touch with her, which have never seen her. But as soon as she is destroyed there is an immediate end to the community as such. Our "ant-catchers" here in the Transvaal never attempt to destroy directly the millions of workers and soldiers in the nest, they take out the queen instead. For every queen they receive a fee of two pounds. Dr. Bugnion, and every observer, must at least become aware of this sustaining power of the queen; if he becomes aware of this, he must realize that she has functions other than merely sexual; that at any rate in this direction she has some psychological function which neither depth nor imprisonment can thwart. From this realization it is only a step further to the discovery of all her psychological functions. With as much reason for objection he might ask: How can an organ like the brain which is shut up in a dark vault, direct and know the functions of the blood corpuscles even in the toes?

One more word about explanation of the origin of the instinct of the termites. He says:

"The origin of most of these instincts is a reasoned and conscious action."

I find it difficult to believe that this explanation could be made seriously today. What would Dr. Bugnion say of hundreds of our South African desert plants which attain all kinds of far-off objectives by the cleverest plans? Have these plants also reasoned and thought in human fashion, thus solved one difficulty after another, and transmitted this knowledge to their descendants?

All this discussion has been caused by the wonderful change which has taken place in the termitary from the time when we

140

saw the queen feeding her young ones and when a few months later we open the palace cell for observation. It is difficult to make clear to the uninitiated reader why this change is so amazing to the psychologist.

In the first instance we were observing an ordinary flying insect at work, behaving in the normal way with normal reactions, except of course the birth-pain and mother-love reactions. Now, at our later observations, a new soul and a new body have appeared. The queen is no longer an insect. She has received a new soul. What has she become? How can one classify her? The biologist who thinks the matter over carefully will find difficulty in finding a place for her in a classified list. The soldiers and workers? The psychologist would say that these too are not insects. He classifies all living organisms according to their behaviour. The workers and soldiers, with only the merest semblance of an individual psyche, fall outside all classes. We are reminded again of the fairy godmother who waves her wand – the pumpkin becomes a coach, the mice prancing steeds.

I find it simple to form an image of the general trend which development took in the case of the termitary. In any case, it seems unnecessary to look for miraculous reasons for this. It is unnecessary to suppose that the termites are capable of talking, thinking, acting and remembering in human fashion. One would have expected an observer to find the simplest explanation first. Dr. Bugnion's demonstration shows us that this is not always the case. His two theories are based on the hypothesis that the termites are simply small humans to whom "an exchange of ideas" is possible. The queen, before her flight, walks round the nest, and comes into touch with

141

the workers and soldiers. She studies their community life and there is "an exchange of ideas". From this point Dr. Bugnion becomes more and more difficult to understand. What he appears to mean is that the queen remembers the lessons she learnt from the workers and soldiers, and although she never herself takes part in their labours, although she herself never shows any signs of the specialized instinct which animate the workers and soldiers, yet in spite of this she transmits these lessons to her offspring. According to Dr. Bugnion the queen does something which man has not succeeded in doing. Man does not transmit a single acquired memory to his progeny. The son of the greatest mathematician does not inherit even the multiplication table.

This theory savours too much of magic. Dr. Bugnion found himself in very deep water. There is not a single fact or condition in nature or in the life history of the termite which justified his opinion. It must have been pure inspiration. There is one great difficulty which Dr. Bugnion never saw, for he leaves it unmentioned. Suppose his theory is right, that the queen transmits in this way the special instincts to her offspring. There still remains the problem, how does it happen that the queen gives birth to two kinds of insect which resemble her as little as a scorpion does a butterfly? This cannot be due to the lessons she learnt from the soldiers and workers in the original termitary. Why does she transmit the special instincts only to two kinds of young, which do not inherit her own instincts, while she does not transmit these acquired instincts to the third offspring, the potential queens? The last type inherit not only her own physical form, but all her special instincts and not a single one of the instincts of the soldiers and workers. His theory cannot be the true one.

His other theory is that the soldiers and workers were at one time fertile and that the present types are the descendants of soldier and worker ancestors when these were fertile.

I have tried to show before that this is a topsy-turvy assumption which cannot be held. Besides, there still remains the difficulty of explaining how the queen manages to divide her inherited memories, some of which are latent, among her three types of offspring.

Let us compare all this with my own theory. I believe that the termite was originally a single flying insect exposed to all kinds of dangers. To keep her eggs and offspring safe she took refuge in an underground shelter. Here, just as happens with the bee, *Halictus,* she came into touch with her young after they were hatched. This was the beginning of community life.

Finally, to cause the community to function well, there was a division of labour. Some of the insects had to build and look for food, others had to protect the nest. Compare the story of *Siphonophora* mentioned already. The queen who tended to produce offspring more suitable for the various kinds of labour would have a greater chance of survival than one who did not have this tendency. Natural selection began to operate. The present-day soldiers and workers were the fittest types for protection and building operations and the sexual types for reproduction. The queen who had the tendency to produce these three types had more chance of survival and transmitted this tendency to the females born from her. Natural selection thus operated in two directions. The nearer the workers and soldiers came physically to the present-day types, the more chance had the community of surviving. A queen was selected naturally, therefore, who gave birth to all three types. Finally a queen and king were selected who not only produced these three types, but who possessed the psychological power to influence the community and to take the place of the individual instincts of the workers and soldiers.

It is easy to understand why it was an advantage to the community for the sexual sense to be destroyed in all types. Even the sexual types (potential kings and queens) possess no sexuality while they remain in the termitary. Sex in such a community would have been a disturbing influence which would have suspended all protective and other work over long periods. In order to do the best and ceaseless labour, the workers and soldiers had to become mere automata governed by the psychological power of the queen. For the same reason, they lost their sight and the other senses which are the accompaniment of an individual psyche. The soldiers and workers therefore inherit no special instincts from their parents. It is the queen who inherits the power of transmitting the semblance of such instincts to the automatons who work for her.

13

THE WATER SUPPLY

I n many parts of the world we find people studying the life-history of termites. In spite of this, no single observer seems to have discovered the psychological functions of the queen, but, more surprising still, no one seems to have realized the intriguing mystery of the constant supply of water of the termite. M. Barthellier, a Frenchman, has studied the termite in Indo-China, in districts probably as dry as Waterberg. An Englishman, Carpenter, studied certain termites for a long time in British East Africa; Maxwell Le Roy in India; Prell, a German, in German East Africa; the Belgians Hegh and Ghesguière in the Congo; Hill in Australia; and many others in parts of North and South America. The collected works of all these observers and many others would fill a library. Yet none of them ever sought to answer the questions:

1. Why does community life of soldiers and workers cease when the queen is destroyed? and
2. Where do the termites get their water?

The very facts seem to have escaped their notice: the never-ceasing supply of water during the dryest seasons, and the change of behaviour caused by the destruction of the queen. If one fails to notice these things, of course, the problems and unavoidable investigation of them will not arise. I want to describe my own observations on the conveyance of water. I was much impressed at the time by the result of my observations and also the effect they had on the other spectators. I think the behaviour of these people was as interesting as the behaviour of the termites. It was sheer chance which gave me the opportunity of watching for months the terrific struggle – it was verily struggle between life and death – unfold itself like a film on the screen. It was during the most severe drought which had ever stricken the Waterberg. That none such had occurred within human memory was certain, for on the farm Rietfontein 1638, where my observations took place, a sixty-year-old orange grove was entirely destroyed by the drought. Nature showed by many signs that it was the peak of a period of drought which had been gradually but systematically increasing for over three hundred years.

Just behind the farmhouse on Rietfontein was a range of hills which divided the farm in half. On the brow of the range were innumerable castles of the Waterberg termite. Many of these termitaries had been dead for some time but just as many were, during the very worst of the drought, alive and intact. I had often before pondered over their secret water supply, but at this time it became a bewildering riddle to me. The whole atmosphere was so dry that even at night there was not the least semblance of dew.

The whole surface of the farm was intersected with canals and ditches, and it could be confirmed by careful examination that along the range there was no trace of water in the earth to a depth of forty feet. With really hard labour we opened two termitaries situated on the summit of the hills. In one we found an eight-foot cobra* which covered old Mr. Gys van Rooyen and myself with venom. Both of us received it full in the face, but luckily our eyes escaped.

In both these termitaries the palace cavity was six feet below the surface of earth as hard as a rock. Yet the whole of the palace cavity and the fungus gardens were moist. In the palace cavity the temperature was two degrees above the normal blood temperature of the human. Water vapour was present in all the passages. The queen and all her subjects appeared to be perfectly normal.

The only unusual feature we found was that many of the gardens near the palace had dried up. Where did the termites obtain their water? I must confess that I came eventually to the solemn conviction, that the termites in some way or other manufactured water from oxygen and hydrogen. Where they obtained the hydrogen was another inexplicable mystery. But I knew the termites were capable of many wonderful things and my solution seemed the only possible one.

I first came on the track of the truth through an account given me by Mr. Jan Wessel Wessels, one of the finest of practical naturalists. He told me that while he was living in Bechuanaland he had twice observed in wells vertical canals made by the termites to incredible depths in order to reach water. Even this I felt was a solution which was difficult to accept.

* The "ringhals", or "ringneck", of the Boers, *Naja nigricollis,* which has the power of spitting its venom to range of about six feet. It aims at the eyes and is very accurate.

The termites on the range at Rietfontein would have had to go down vertically to a depth of at least a hundred feet to obtain water.

Then again all our attempts to find the beginning of such an aqueduct were unsuccessful. Later we discovered the reason for this. It was only the widely known and undoubted trustworthiness of Mr. Wessels which allowed me to accept the explanation as the true one. Then mere chance ordained that I myself was able to see the whole business functioning.

In this terrible drought, it was not only the termites who were seeking for water, but we humans too. On the brow of the aforementioned range was a clump of green bushes which contrasted agreeably with the parched veld. Mr. Van Rooyen thought there must be water at this spot and his belief was upheld by a water diviner. Men immediately began excavating a square pit in the centre of the green clump. When the pit was about forty feet deep I was told by the labourers that a termite runway was visible on the north wall for its whole depth, and I lost no time in going to the spot to study the amazing work, in detail. The first fact I established was that the termitary connected with this canal was at least thirty feet away from the pit. I exposed the whole tunnel and also part of the gardens adjacent to the palace cavity. The latter I covered with a wooden lid, to enable me to observe them from time to time. I then discovered that the aqueduct did not descend vertically from the nest, but from the end of a long horizontal passage. This was the reason for our failing to discover it in the termitaries we opened.

I was then enabled also to discover a fact in relation to termite behaviour which would have helped me to infer the exis-

Termite runways on a tree

tence of a shaft into the depths, before actually seeing one, if only I had been able to reason clearly. When the ground is wet, in rainy seasons, the workers always begin repairing any damage to the outer crust immediately. In dry seasons, however, it takes hours, sometimes days, before the builders make their appearance and tackle the work. No wonder, if each little worker has to descend hundreds of feet to get his masonry. But this solution escaped me. I simply did not think of it!

Another noteworthy point in connection with the vertical shaft was that in one plane, north and south, there were absolutely no bends. In the other plane, east and west, there were many unnecessary bends. This meant that the shaft was visible through its whole length on the north wall of the well, in spite of the turnings east and west. The vertical direction in one plane was of course a great labour-saving to the termites; but why did they not make the borehole absolutely vertical? Their method, like everything else they do, appeared almost but not absolutely perfect. They are extremely wise in some ways and so very stupid in others.

It is possible that the magnetic poles of the earth may have had an influence on this work of the termites. In Australia is found a certain termite, the Magnetic White Ant, which builds an elongated termitary with the longer axis pointing north and south. In their case there is no doubt that building is determined by the magnetic poles of our sphere. So remarkable are the bends occurring only in one plane in the aqueduct of our termites that for the present we may accept the theory that the perpendicularity in one plane is due to the magnetism of the earth. East and West there is no magnetic power to keep the termites in the vertical direction. Every two

150

or three feet in the shaft was situated a small white garden patch, dry and unplanted. It should not be forgotten, however, that I probably never saw more than half of the shaft. At a depth of forty feet, the well was abandoned because the ground even there was still as dry as a bone, whereas Mr. Van Rooyen and the water diviner had thought a plentiful supply would be found at twenty-five feet. The distance of the nest from the bottom of the well was sixty-five feet, and here the shaft disappeared into the earth. There is no doubt that there were live gardens deeper down and nearer the water.

I constantly examined workers coming up the shaft under the microscope and nearly all of them had hyphae, seed ready for planting, in their bodies. During my observation I came to certain conclusions:

1. That the community could not exist a single day in the terrible drought without water.
2. That this could be the only shaft by which water was conveyed; for even for workers like the termites it would take years to reach that depth.
3. That they were forced to use this shaft in spite of their intense aversion to light.

It was impossible for them to make a new shaft, and there was no chance of covering in the old shaft, for haste, haste and haste again had to be the war-cry of the termites in the terrific struggle in which they were engaged.

In the end I was proved correct in all my conclusions. It was one of the few times when one could prophesy with certainty. I had the opportunity of watching their struggle for existence for months and of learning and understanding step by step all that was happening. During this time I visited the shaft at all hours of the day and night from sunset to sunrise, and never for one moment did I discover any cessation of the infinite labour. Nor was there even the least slackening. Once I marked a number of workers with aniline blue and could establish the fact that they never rested or slept, that they worked day and night, that the same workers who were marked by day were busy at night climbing up and down.

It is noteworthy that in the beginning I did not get the impression of haste and alarm which I received so clearly some time later. There were two streams of workers, those on the right going down, those on the left going up, and this order was maintained to the very last. The two streams were in single file, with a distance of about two inches separating each termite from the next one. The workers I marked took, in the beginning, about half an hour to reach the end of the shaft and return to the nest with their load from the depths. Later on this period shortened until it became about twenty minutes.

I then became aware that the whole character of the activity was changing. There was a slowly increasing concentration on the aqueduct, the streams of termites became thicker and thicker, and I got an impression of general consternation. It took me a long time to discover the real reason for this. I could see they were occupied with some task which taxed the energy and power of resistance of the community to the utmost. What exactly did it signify? There was a complete cessation of any repair work. No attempt was made to cover over the shaft. A breach made in the termitary was simply ignored, while all workers and soldiers in the neighbourhood disappeared. After a week or ten days a meagre cordon of soldiers appeared at the edge of the wound, and then sporadic attempts at repair were made by the workers. The necessary building materials were brought from the depths of the shaft. My own inference was that all the disturbance and heightened circulation was concentrated on the palace cavity, and that the object of it was to convey water to the queen, larvae and soldiers. I knew that the queen was merely a bag of liquid; that she laid on an average one hundred and fifty thousand eggs every twenty-four hours, and that for the purposes of all her functions she must require a constant and copious supply of water, while ninety per cent of the bodies of the rest of the termites consisted of water.

But the provision of water to the living termites was not the only reason for this quickened pulse. When I exposed the outer gardens, I noticed there, on a line dividing the gardens in two, there was a constantly crawling throng of termites. I had forgotten that for the king and queen, for larvae and soldiers, these gardens were just as necessary as a water supply. The gardens, as I explained before, are digestive organs without which the community could not exist for even one day.

All the above-mentioned types are entirely dependent on the gardens, for the workers are the only type which can make use of partially digested food. The gardens are the stomach and the liver of the composite animal. The workers are the mouth and teeth. Long and very careful observation was necessary to enable me to understand what the enormous concentration on the gardens meant. At last I noticed that all the gardens external to the line I have mentioned were parched and that this death of the gardens was creeping inward from day to day. It was on this line dividing the dead gardens from the living that I found the greatest concentration of activity. It took the form of a terrific onslaught, engaged in with such fury that the workers and soldiers could spare no moment for rest. It was a mighty struggle against death's stealthy approach; there was no respite for the defenders day or night.

The workers were engaged in replanting hyphae round the living gardens, and in irrigating these freshly planted seeds; and every little seed, every drop of moisture had to be carried a hundred feet out of the depths of the earth. Sixty-five feet of this distance was visible to me. During the night the defenders would gain ground. During this cool period when evaporation was at its lowest ebb the line would be pushed outwards a half or a quarter of an inch. During the heat of the day, however, the enemy would press heavily and gain the hardly won advance.

It was at night, during the hours when the rest of nature was quietest, that the fierceness of the fight gained most frenzy. I could hear distinctly the unceasing alarm calls of the soldiers, a sound which roused even in me a feeling of terrible anxiety. My electric searchlight revealed the restless stream constantly passing to and fro, as sure and indomitable as fate itself. Nothing could turn them from their purpose, no external terror could distract them. The death of a thousand individuals made not the least impression on that living stream. Vaguely and faintly, I began to realize, as I watched, what the struggle for existence really means in nature.

14

THE FIRST ARCHITECTS

I suppose every investigator of termite classification or behaviour must at one time or another have been dumbfounded by the ambitious nature of their building and engineering operations. The mightiest structures man has built on this earth; the pyramids of Egypt, London's underground system, New York's skyscrapers, the Simplon tunnel, the biggest cathedrals, the longest bridges, these, compared with works of the termite, taking into consideration its size, are as molehills compared with mountains.

Wilhelm Bölsche, in *Der Termieten Staat,* made some calculations to show how the work of man compares with that of the termite. Taking size into consideration, man would have to erect a building as high as the Matterhorn, that is 14,760 feet, if his work was to be equal to a termite tower forty feet in height, such as is often found in Africa. Such was the estimate of the German writer. It is not the size of the termitary only, however, which amazes the investigator, but the almost incredible extent of their underground activity.

I have already described at some length their vertical boreholes, those mighty feats of engineering which they have been forced to carry out in their ceaseless struggle against drought.

They are forced to penetrate the bowels of the earth in their eternal search for water, which they have to convey drop by drop in order to keep their large communities from death. The actual depth of these shafts we do not know; the one I have mentioned before was deeper – exactly how much deeper is uncertain – than sixty-five feet.

I want to give an account of some facts which came to my knowledge when I made a journey through the valley of the Limpopo and the Lowveld of Zoutpansberg a few years ago.

It was during this journey that I came to a real appreciation of the astounding genius for building which the termites possess. Everyone who is interested in the termite will have read and probably seen photographs of the enormous termitaries which are found in tropical parts of Africa. In the Lowveld of Zoutpansberg I found some giants, nor were these the exception by any means. In some parts of the Limpopo valley these gigantic termitaries are a very usual feature of the landscape. An engineer friend of mine, Norman Hugel, carefully measured and calculated the weight of earth making up one colossus, and found that it consisted of eleven thousand seven hundred and fifty tons of earth. This termitary belonged to a small *Eutermes*. Just think of it, eleven thousand seven hundred tons which had been piled up grain by grain, for *Eutermes* never uses mud for building purposes. They use only microscopic grains of sand; every one is rubbed clean and polished before being coated in a sticky cement; then every tiny stone is carefully placed in the right place. So grain by grain, the termites heaped up a structure weighing eleven thousand seven hundred tons. One would imagine it to take thousands of years to accomplish, but it was hopeless to try to

156

estimate the period of time. There is no doubt that it was a matter of centuries. There is yet another mystery connected with this particular activity of the termites, which I cannot recollect ever to have seen mentioned by other observers. The riddle is simply this: From where does the enormous mass of earth come? One would expect to find a hollow cavity below such a vast excrescence; a hollow in the earth corresponding in size to the superficial mass, because there is no doubt that all the building material is carried from below. No signs of any cavity have ever been found, however, notwithstanding the fact that many of the giants have been intersected in many parts of Africa and have even been totally demolished for purposes of road-making, railway lines, house building, dams, aerodromes and all the many activities to which civilized man is prone.

For instance, in order to level the surface of the Bulawayo aerodrome alone, twenty thousand tons of "ant-heap" were carted away. In all such cases, especially for purposes of making railways, dams or heavy buildings, the ground is always carefully tested for cavities after the surface termitaries have been removed; yet no hollows corresponding in size to the superficial structures have ever been found. Yet we know that the building material of the termites must come out of the earth.

The reader will remember how I discovered the source of the termite water supply by sheer chance, after it had been to me for many years such an unsolved problem that I had come to the conclusion that the insects manufactured water from hydrogen and oxygen.

I believe now that if I had given the matter more thought

A tower termitary.

A pagoda, or mushroom, termitary.

and reasoned more clearly, these giant termitaries with no cavities below them would have led me to the truth. In the first place millions of gallons of water were necessary to build these structures, and a further inexhaustible supply for the needs of the termites themselves and the internal economy of the vast termitary. A quite considerable stream of water must flow into the nest day and night to keep alive the community. The explanation stares one in the face: Both water and building material come from innumerable tiny cavities in the earth, which the termites are constantly increasing, for the purpose of enlarging the termitary and their water supply as the community grows. It seems a kind of vicious circle.

In another instance I found a rocky kopje or hill in the Sabie Valley, which consisted of one vast termitary belonging to the much-feared *Macrotermes bellicosus,* the Fighting Termite. The bite of the bloodthirsty soldiers of M. *bellicosus* goes deep enough to cause considerable bleeding. One of these soldiers I took back to Pretoria with me and managed to keep alive for a week after his separation from the nest. He could bite right through the wood of a matchbox with a crunch which was distinctly audible at a distance of four or five yards. This termitary, comprising as it did a whole kopje, caused me a great deal of mystification. I simply could not accept for one moment the notion that the huge rocks on its summit had been heaved up by the building operations of the termites. It is true that Dr. Preller and I found stones weighing ten and twelve pounds high up in the termitaries of *Eutermes* at Pelindaba, which could only have got there through elevation by the termites. But on the kopje were rocks hundreds of tons in weight. Every inch of ground between and under these rocks consisted of the pebble-built structures of *M. bellicosus*. The probable solution was that the termites had first removed all the original earth between the rocks and then substituted their own pebble work.

I had never seen anything like this occurring however, and the question of what they had done with all the original earth still remained. For there was no sign of normal earth.

I have mentioned this case merely as an illustration of the countless insoluble problems which constantly confront the investigator.

During this journey I took the opportunity of doing some experiments to find out in what way and how far magnetism affects the termite. Mr. Piet Haak of Pretoria kindly lent me a dozen of the strongest steel magnets obtainable. I speedily became convinced, however, that my magnetic field was too weak. To come to any certain conclusion, a powerful electro-magnet would have to be used. I have no doubt, however, that the magnetic force of the earth influences the work of all termites. In this connection, one should remember the water-shaft at Waterberg which had bends only east and west.

The "compass termites" of Australia build their termitaries with the narrowest diameter towards the magnetic north. The late Mr. Claude Fuller alleged that the summits of the termitaries of *M. bellicosus* always leant towards the true west.

In the Lowveld we established the fact that the termitaries of *M. bellicosus* were always narrower in one plane than the other. A straight line through the widest diameter always pointed true east and west. In the neighbourhood of these last-mentioned termitaries there was a palm tree of 160 feet in height. Quite by chance I found a covered-in termite runway going up the trunk and vanishing in the foliage above. On investigation we found that this passage was used by *Eutermes* workers for the purpose of fetching water from the top of the palm to their termitary, which was sixty feet away from the foot of the tree. I took the opportunity during this time, too, of studying the art of the *Eutermes* builders in more detail, and while observing the building I found the subject of nutrition constantly looming large. Claude Fuller and other famous observers call *Eutermes* the Haymakers, and take it for granted that the grass collected by these termites is used for food. When one examines a termitary belonging to *Eutermes,* one finds that many passages are filled with dry grass stalks of about half an inch in length. This grass is carried to the termitary at night through passages which spread out in all directions. At intervals in these passages there are storerooms where some of the grass is carefully stowed and even actually inside the termitary there are sometimes parts filled to such an extent with grass that there is barely room for soldiers and workers to pass. "Food" says my friend Claude Fuller and "Food" bay the other observers, without any doubt arising in their minds.

It must be food, they decide, because such a large quantity is stored and so much of their activity is centred on collecting it. There could have been no other basis for their conclusion, though no one has ever seen *Eutermes* eating grass, nor has anyone found grass within the body of the termite.

I myself threw this theory overboard many years ago. I convinced myself by microscopic examinations that *Eutermes* was not equipped for chewing grass and swallowing it; I doubt very much whether the worker could do this. Its mouth

162

parts certainly are more developed than those of the soldier, but this development is directed towards special functions – the conveyance of grains of sand, coating them with sticky fluid, the feeding of fluids to the queen and larvae, and severing grass stalks. But they are quite incapable, it seems to me, of masticating and swallowing the latter. Another reason which made me question the food theory was because I never succeeded in finding under the microscope the least sign of grass in the entrails of the workers or soldiers. All that I found was a fluid which had every appearance of being derived from the moisture of the earth and the sap of plant roots.

Later I learnt of certain observations in South America which strengthened my conclusions. I have mentioned before that the habits of ants and termites are often so much alike, that the behaviour of one affords a key to the behaviour of the other.

In South America and Mexico there is an ant known as the leaf-cutting ant, which does great damage to trees by cutting round pieces from the leaves. These they drop to the ground where other workers are waiting to pounce on them and bear them to the nest. Without any further investigation, it was assumed that these leaves were used for food. Recently, however, an observer in Mexico proved that the leaves are never used for feeding purposes. Instead they are packed in masses on the side of the nest where the heat of the sun is most fierce. The theory of this observer is that the leaves serve the sole purpose of protection against the rays of the tropical sun. Whether this is so, we cannot say, but at all events the leaves are not eaten and do not serve as food. I then wondered whether *Eutermes* might be using grass for the same purpose.

163

Eutermes workers building an arch by gradual approximation of two pillars.

I soon realized, however, that this could not be the case, for the method of storing would not enable the grass to serve as a protection.

Now all the architecture of *Eutermes* is based on the arch. Probably they were the first architects to discover the secret of arch building. It took years of civilization before man discovered how to use the arch in architecture. Those mighty builders, the Egyptians, knew nothing of the arch and limited themselves to two vertical pillars with a colossal stone as crossbeam. The Greeks and Romans did not understand the properties of the arch. It was only in the Middle Ages that

164

Eutermes workers building an arch. In this case a grass stalk is laid from pillar to pillar, and covered with tiny pebbles.

architects came to understand fully the value of the arch in building.

It is very interesting to note that we find in the architecture of the termite two stages of development of the arch, analogous to that in human architecture.

Let us return to *Eutermes* and examine some new building operations after rain has fallen. One portion of the termitary has a dark stain. If we examine this with a magnifying glass we find that it is a wet patch where the outer crust has disappeared. It is possible to cut away a small piece of this without causing enough disturbance to make the workers disappear.

165

Now we can examine the building of the first architects of this earth. We see that all the building of *Eutermes* is based on the arch. This arch is formed in two ways; the first and most primitive is made by inclining two vertical pillars towards each other until they meet. This is the way man, too, made his first arch. But about every eighth worker carries in his mouth a grass-stalk instead of a pebble. He ascends one of the pillars, quickly fastens one end of the stalk with sticky fluid to the top of the pillar, and then rushes away without waiting to see what happens. This is what does happen: The grass-stalk sinks slowly towards the other pillar until its end comes to rest on the summit. There we see another worker waiting in readiness. As soon as the end of the stalk comes within his reach, he stretches up, grips it, and pulls it down to the summit of the pillar where he in turn attaches it with fluid. On this crossbeam the termites plaster tiny pebbles until a perfect arch results. Success is by no means always inevitable. Occasionally the stalk remains vertical instead of sinking down. In these cases the termites simply finish the arch by inclining the tops of the vertical pillars towards each other until they meet, while the stalk is eventually covered with masonry. Why the stalk is used at all when the termites are able to finish the arch with pebbles only, I cannot tell. Perhaps it is only a rudimentary remainder of a principle which has disappeared. Whatever may be the explanation, I am positive *Eutermes* never uses the grass-stalks as food.

15

THE QUEEN IN HER CELL

It was not until long after I had published most of my observations that I for the first time had an opportunity of investigating at my leisure the most important phenomenon in
the psychological life of the termite. By this I mean the behaviour of the queen, as a living and active part of the community. I had attempted hundreds of times on the veld to expose
the palace cavity in such a manner that the functions of the
queen and what occurs in her immediate vicinity would be
visible to me. I am referring of course to what happens in a
full-grown termitary. I had had the opportunity of watching
the development of a nest, but my observations were of neces-
sity curtailed, and gave no inkling of what happens later when
the queen is sealed in her cell and continues life as the brain
of the community.

An opportunity came my way quite unexpectedly in Pretoria. There was a house in Arloius Lane which had been
infested with termites for years. They were continually causing great destruction and a number of attempts had been
made in vain to rid the house of them. The queen had never
been found and immediately the damage to the house had
been repaired the termites began their work of destruction

anew. At last the Town Council undertook the work of exterminating them. Mr. Victor Foster and I followed with great interest the labours of the workmen while they were trying to track down the queen. After the searchers had tried in vain for many days to find the palace cavity I made a proposal to the foreman. I was convinced that in this case there was only one queen and that the community was not one which was influenced by two or more queens, where the subjects would swear allegiance to another queen if their own were destroyed. I suggested that I would point out the palace cavity on condition that I might observe the living queen for two or three days. To this proposal the foreman agreed. Within a few minutes I had established three main passages and their point of intersection, and was then in a position to point out with a fair degree of accuracy the place where the queen's cell would be found. The palace cavity, luckily for us, was under a hearth in the darkest corner of one of the rooms. Mr. Foster and I exposed this ourselves, with the help of an electric torch. We succeeded in cutting first the palace cavity and then the actual cell of the queen in half without causing any undue disturbance to the community. We simply carved away a portion of the skull and there before us lay the living, functioning brain of the organism. It was indeed a spectacle more wonderful than I had expected. How I regretted we had stipulated for only two or three days!

Some of the phenomena which this exposure revealed to me I was acquainted with, and for these I watched. Others came as complete surprises, and revealed amazing secrets. This was what we saw. The queen was enormously big, and lay with her body pointing east and west, her head towards the west. The king, who of course was only the usual size of the flying termite, was constantly either on her gigantic body or in its immediate neighbourhood. There was nothing in his behaviour which could in any way establish his function, although I made detailed notes on his every movement. A large mass of the smaller class of worker was in constant movement on the queen and around her. Immediately in front of the head of the queen was a small opening which served as entrance and exit and which was, of course, far too small for the queen to pass through. Through this small opening two streams of workers were constantly passing, one stream coming in and another going out. We very soon established the fact that these small workers were occupied with three different tasks:

1. One stream was engaged in feeding the queen. Each worker stopped close to her head, and raised itself in order to reach her mouth. Immediately a tiny drop of clear fluid shining like a diamond appeared in its jaws, to disappear at once into the mouth of the queen. As soon as he had tendered his morsel to his sovereign, the worker walked round her gigantic body, so as to reach the exit on the opposite side from that by which he had entered. The work, therefore, went with the greatest speed and regularity, without any worker ever impeding another unnecessarily.

2. With these workers and in the same streams were some who had the task of carrying away the eggs and caring for them. These workers, too, walked right round the queen, to appear later carrying eggs in the outgoing stream. Mr. Foster calculated that the queen laid fifty thousand eggs in

twenty-four hours, which gives some idea of the speed with which the task of conveying them had to be accomplished.

3. A much smaller group of workers were occupied with a far more mysterious task. I could not find out exactly what they were doing but assumed they were busy cleaning the skin of the queen in some way. They were constantly engrossed, either singly or in groups, in some task on the queen's gigantic body. They appeared to be stroking her skin softly with their jaws in a continuous movement. We did discover that when they entered the cell their bodies were empty, whereas when they left they were filled with a colourless fluid. This fluid must therefore have been obtained in some way through the skin of the queen without in any way damaging it. We called these workers masseurs. It may be that they were appointed to some special work of feeding the young ones and that the queen secreted in her enormous body the fluid used for this purpose. I base this assumption on what we actually saw happening when we followed up some of these masseurs after they had left the queen's cell. This observation, however, I still had some doubt about, for we experienced some difficulty in following up these workers. It appeared, however, that the masseurs after they left the cell visited one of the big breeding gardens, where there were a large number of the small white babies. Here they fed the babies with drops of colourless fluid, in exactly the same way that other workers of this class fed the queen. It occurred to me therefore that the body of the queen served as an organ for digesting food a stage further for use of part of the community. In her body

a change occurs which renders the nutriment fit for infant feeding. If this is actually the case, it is the first appearance in nature of "milk" secretion by the mother. Besides these three classes of workers and their never-ending activity, we observed an even more interesting phenomenon in the palace cavity. The cell of the queen was encircled by a ring of the bigger soldiers. These soldiers were equidistant from each other. The plane of the circle was placed at an angle of approximately forty-five degrees to water-level. In the foreground of the palace cavity the soldiers were standing on the floor, while at the opposite side they were hanging upside down from the roof. All their heads were turned directly to the magnetic north. I think this fact is of importance, because I am convinced that the magnetism of the earth has a noticeable effect on most kinds of termite, as has already been indicated in connection with the water-shaft in Africa and in the shape of the termitaries of the "magnetic ant" of Australia. The members of this body-guard, as we may call it, were, for most of the time, entirely motionless. Every now and then, however, one of them became activated with a curious motion, a swaying to and fro of the head and foremost part of the body, which reminded me of the well-known termite dance described by observers. As soon as one member began these movements he infected within few seconds the soldier nearest him on his right side, who in his turn handed it on to the one next to him and so on from one to another, until the peculiar dance had been transmitted right round the circle, to end where it had begun.

We also saw the changing of the guards. The new guards entered the palace cavity by a large opening nearly opposite the head end of the cell, and formed a second circle within the circle of the guards about to be relieved. The new guards then gradually widened their circle to take their places between the old guards. This was the signal for the latter to leave the cell in single file by the same opening. This was the only activity we observed on the part of these soldiers.

What could be the function of this mysterious circle? Another observer, who later had the opportunity of seeing them in German West Africa, describes them with the utmost assurance as real bodyguards which fulfil the same function as royal bodyguards do in the case of a human sovereign. I am afraid I cannot accept this theory. Any enemy which had succeeded in penetrating the nest thus far, would surely be capable of overcoming this single line very easily. One must remember that such an enemy would have come through miles of passages where he would meet countless soldiers of the same class, who would, *à outrance,* withstand every inch of his approach with every means of attack and defence. If he had succeeded in forcing his way thus far, no mere circle of bodyguards would be the slightest use. I may add that I never succeeded in stirring up this bodyguard to attack. I could touch them with my finger and move them from side to side, without any of them making the least attempt to bite, which any other soldier of the same class would have done immediately in any other part of the nest. They appeared to me to be semi-conscious like chloroformed termites.

I immediately formulated another theory. The termitary is

such a perfect analogy to the physical body of an animal with its brain, its stomach and liver, its blood-stream consisting of two kinds of corpuscles, that I am inclined to clarify any unknown phenomenon in the termite by comparison with higher animals. It had always appeared to me that there was one analogous organ lacking in the termitary. I had always felt that there should be some system with a similar function linking up the community and its "brain", the queen, as is found in the central nervous system of animals. I had always been searching for something which would be the functional equivalent of the *medulla oblongata* and the vertebral column; which would act as a link to carry the mysterious influence of the queen to all parts of the community. I must admit that this is a theory which is supported by very few observations. I am giving it here for what it may be worth. Perhaps future observers will have the opportunity of investigating this mysterious circle more thoroughly and establishing its functions. Of one thing we may be certain, that such a complicated and regular phenomenon must have some definite purpose.

I must describe another occurrence which took place during our observation because it bears upon the theory of the organic unity of the termitary.

While we were watching the queen, a fairly large piece of hard clay became detached from the edge of the roof of the cell and fell down, dealing the queen a somewhat hard blow. Immediately a series of extraordinary occurrences took place. The only effect which the shock had on the queen herself, was that she began moving her head to and fro in a rhythmic fashion. The workers immediately ceased all work within the cell and wandered round in aimless groups. The circle of bodyguards broke up at once and most of them vanished down the passages behind the palace cavity. Then we saw masses of tiny workers thronging into the palace cavity and cell. They swarmed over the queen in order to suck the fluid through her skin, in exactly the same way as the masseurs had done in normal circumstances. The king greedily took part in this draining of his mate. They succeeded so well that within a few minutes the skin of the queen was hanging in loose folds.

In the meantime we visited far outlying parts of the nest, where the termites had been very active just before the accident. Even in the farthest parts all work had ceased. The large soldiers and workers gathered in great excitement in different parts of the nest. There appeared to be a tendency to collect in groups. There was not the least doubt the shock to the queen was felt in the outermost parts of the termitary within a few minutes. Recovery began in the same place where the first and greatest disturbance took place. Slowly the destructive workers stopped their assault on the queen. The bodyguards took up their positions in a circle and the queen ceased the rhythmic movements of her head. She appeared to be recovering from the shock. So quickly that it was barely possible for me to follow all the stages, normal activity began anew. The only difference in conduct which I could notice was that the workers appeared to be speeding up the feeding of the queen, and before long her body had resumed its usual gigantic size. The following day all activity in the outermost parts of the termitary was in full swing.

174

And that was the end of our observations.

The workmen had occupied themselves with excavating and removing the breeding gardens in other rooms, but now the time allotted to us had come to an end. The queen was removed from her half-cell and taken away captive; and after that the activities and life of this nest ceased for good.